D0710772

Between The Tides

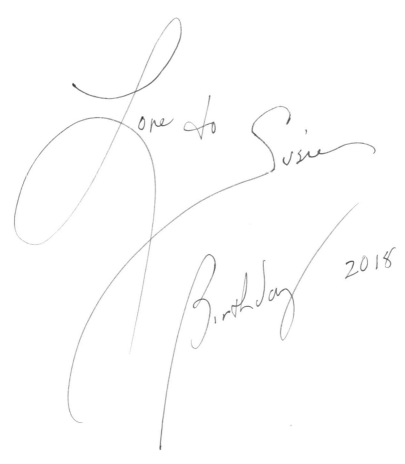

Love to Susie

Birthday 2018

Between The Tides

~ POEMS OF THE CAPE & ISLANDS ~

John P. Joy

© Copyright John P. Joy 2016
All rights reserved.

ISBN-13: 9781539564201
ISBN-10: 1539564207

For Sara

Table of Contents

Coast Lines

Sweet Summer Is A Comin' In

Sweet summer is acomin' in,
Loudly sing Cape Cod,
Groweth ease and bloweth breeze,
Warmeth the waters new,
Sing Cape Cod now,

Mothers bleateth after their lambs,
Displayeth now their tan-ned gams,
Their bucks do leapeth, expelleth air,
Merrily sing her Islands fair,

Merrily sing Cape & Islands,
You singeth well, maketh no farewell,
Sing Cape Cod now, sing Islands now,
Loudly sing Cape & Islands,
Sing Cape & Islands now.

Sibling Coasts

New England boasts two sibling coasts,
Its northern, square jawed, wild and stark,
Full of mystery and implied threat,
Fronting a cold, navy blue ocean,
Edged with rocks, cliffs and lofty pines,
Stingy with sand and the easy view,
Glowering in its nor'easters, monastic,
Standoffish, taciturn, devoid of subtlety,
Home to proper storms, its primary colors
Clear and crisp, full of bravery, male,
Fond of clear lines, marked delineations,
Its mariners in full, rugged sail
Upon her windy bays and gulf,
Exquisitely beautiful all the same,
All Yang, be glad you came,

Its southern, down the Cape,
Tamer, more temperate,
Enchanting beyond word craft
And the laboring scribe's apt metaphor,
Testing our tolerance for charm,
Quaint enough to cause alarm,
Subtler in appeal, nuanced,
Full of gradations, easy transitions,
Pastel coloration and panoramic views,
All seduction, siren song,
Its sedative sands stretching for miles
While like a coastal coquette
She more subtly beguiles,
All Yin, welcome her dainty beauty in,

I think the north is masculine truth,
The south pure feminine beauty,
That it's every visitor's high summer duty
To each embrace, conjoin the two,
To gain a rounded coastal view.

New England Gems

Ruby skies enchanting late day eyes
On the Cape & Islands,
Her sapphire sea, majestic frieze
Between the cornice of the sky
And the architrave of the land,
Palladium skies that surprise
With sudden rains,
Black pearl winter nights
Speckled with 24 karat lights,
Opalescent rainbows,
Pure gold of her summer sun,
Her sterling silver moon,
Beveled edge of her northern coast,
Inlaid with jade, coniferous forests,
Nothing semiprecious,
Nothing of fool's gold,
Resplendent solitaires though,
If you should go,
Available in any setting
In the multifaceted, northeast kingdom
Of flawless, precious New England.

Come Feast Your Eyes

Come feast your eyes
On my shoreline, verdant fields,
Myriad strands, boats well-keeled,
My sand as soft as babies' bums,
Soothing surf that never numbs,
My seafood, tender, broiled or fried,
My seacoast charms on every side,
My beauties, subtle, light and bold,
My colors, turquoise, crimson, gold,
My creatures, gorgeous, varied, free,
My towns astride the splendid sea,
My scented nights, sun-drenched days,
Picture perfect coves and bays,
Come feast your eyes on Cape & Isles,
Where every hallowed inch beguiles.

Cast Off

Cast off your city carapace,
Your matted, urban feathers,
Your hectic life, the old rat race,
All the culture's tethers,
Slough off too
Your scales and skin,
Exuviate, exfoliate,
Let ocean time begin,
Strip away the false façades,
The envelope, the sheathe,
Professional personas,
Let your spirit breathe,
Let fall the weight of winter,
Molt, drop, shed and peel,
From your swelled, egoic mind
A few prized hours steal,
Untie first your bowline,
Loosen next the stern,
Then every fastener, every cleat,
Feel the free soul burn.

Be Shipwrecked

Come to the coast she whispers,
See how the resplendent sun
Now rises over my storied peninsula
And magical islands
Rich with natural enticements,
Illuminating my impeccable contours,
Rousing my countless creatures,
Tugging at your beleaguered soul
And leaden spirit,
Offering sybaritic delights,
Wondrous views,
A bewildering variety of wildlife,
Beckoning blue depths and soothing swells,
Cavort here, gambol, play, make hay
While my happy sun shines all the day,
Make yourself a haven here, a seaside sanctuary,
Make me your restorative, your elixir, your
Cure all, rest with me unperturbed, undetected,
Luxuriate in my seaside amenities,
My formidable beauties,
Sail my tranquil bays and cozy inlets,
Cruise my handsome harbors,
Rest quiescent on my voluptuous sands,
Admire my prideful dunes and lime-green marshes
Festooned with dancing sea grass,
Saunter along my bountiful beaches,
Reclaim your life and your loves,

Be shipwrecked,
Don't squander your brief life with busyness,
Look how my amiable sun already climbs higher,
Witness how this luminous day
Moves relentlessly on, without you.

Such A Tonic

New England is preoccupied
With goals and much achievement,
Yet if we are not careful
Such things may cause bereavement,
We measure life and all our worth
From things we have obtained,
Things we have, things we want,
Ambition unrestrained,
We value time not for itself
But for the space provided,
Within which space we might obtain
What soul might find misguided,
Yet there's the beach,
There's the shore,
A heretic and more,
Putting the lie to our beliefs,
What our brief life is for,
How ironic such a tonic
Surrounds so close at hand,
To give us pause, give us rest,
Gently reprimand.

Faint Call Of An Absent Love

Like the faint call of an absent love
Sounding in a lover's ear,
The Cape & Islands call to me
Through the long and lengthening year,
Each dawdling day, each weary week,
Of coastal charms I hear them speak,
In muffled, teasing, tempting tone,
While by duty yet constrained
I plod in tedious pace alone,
Yet unlike love that's unrequited,
Once their fetching forms are sighted,
In mutual measure love returns,
As year on year they decline to spurn
Even those of one-week stands
Sunning now on lesser strands,
Far beyond Cape's flexed arms reach,
Traitors on some foreign beach,
They know I am the faithful one,
Their seaside swain, beachy beau,
Who's courting has not of late begun,
Who even craves their undertow,
They whisper to me of wicked waves,
The salt sea marsh, the wind-filled sail,
Yet stifled in my city cell
I answer back the worker's wail,
Hush soft, seductive voice I say,
Must you stalk me so?
Why so needy, pinup girls?
I will return you know,
The heart you won in summertime
Beats yet beneath the winter snow.

Listen

Listen, she is calling,
Through the long, hard months
Of somber, dark and drear,
Be still and you will hear,
If you do she'll pull you through
Sad autumn, vile winter, tardy spring,
And one day your depleted spirit bring
Again to life, with
The joy and ease you left behind
When high summer ended,
And spirit in full retreat
Deferred to mind,

Listen, she is calling,
Her velvety voice muffled
By rustling leaves, driven snow,
Damnable, dormant bulbs and seeds
That will not grow,
Though every weary heart wills it so,

So what that winter has its charms?
Who cares for briefest fall?
Spring's a tease that never comes,
Must we love them all?

Listen, she is calling,
Bend low,
Hear your name tenderly spoken,
Here, deep beneath the ceaseless snow,
The call of one you've come to know.

Certainty Of
Another Summer

Amazing things:
The matchless beauty of the shore,
The shock of betrayal by intimates,
The abiding fear of death,
The profundity of synchronicities,
The ubiquity of random kindnesses,
Blue oceans that girdle the world
Yet remain in place even upside down,
The decency of people and, too often,
The indecency of their governments,
The proliferation of unanswered questions,
The transcendence of letting go,
The rootedness of core beliefs,
The centrality of self-compassion,
The alignment of culture and morality,
The daily challenge of taming the mind,
The certainties of the narrow-minded,
The eternal grappling of ego and self,
The seduction of appearances,
The power of words and actions,
The greater power of silence and restraint,
The dominance of humility over arrogance,
The insecurities in every person,
The inestimable value of peace of mind,
The folly of expectations,
The litany of disappointments,
The eye-filling beauty of the human form,
The habit of evil to parade in the garb of the good,

The nobility of some in a wide, dark universe,
The centrality of love,
The ethereal scent of neonates, and
The certainty of another summer.

Cape & Islands Rap No. 1

I need the Cape, can't you tell?
Wicked waves that cast a spell,
Make you well,
Take me there, I'll pay the fare,
Ain't no truth or dare,
What else can compare?
Need some dune, ain't too soon,
A great white for a lark, after I park,
And in the dark swim with the seals
When night congeals,
And nasty sharks are lookin' for meals,
Don't dare doubt me, try to flout me,
Cause you'll be hearin' more about me,
I wanna eat a lobsta roll, take the helm,
Be in control, sail a bit, row a boat,
Cross that big, wide, mother moat,
You mean the canal? that's the one,
Once across I'll grab some sun,
Hook some looks with all this bling,
Cuddle while the shorebirds sing,
Got to get a suit, some sun block,
Learn to talk the seacoast talk,
Walk the walk, forget the clock,
No more of that tick-tock, tick-tock,
Comb the beach, find some shells,
Hang with all the famous swells,
Don't pester me, sequester me,
Try to get the best of me,
I mean to go put on a show,

Eat fried fish, make a wish, get my tan,
Be the man, you know I can,
Ain't no fake out, I mean to get some take out,
Stakin' out my piece of the beach,
It's what I'm here to preach.

I Crave The Sea

I crave the sea, the sky, a view,
More thoughts of you, of nature,
Less of them, of him, of her,
My druthers, less of others,
I yearn to look within, down,
Farther down, up too,
Tell you what I find,
Where I go when out of mind,
Where I left the rushing stream
To dream,

I require more sun, softer rain,
Less of all your pain,
More mountain lakes, waterfalls,
Silent nights, silent days,
More monastic getaways,
More wild things,
Less of what success brings,
Less distraction, interaction,

I cannot feed the multitudes,
Fathom others moods,
Make a bed, see the kids are fed,
Do the town or hide a frown,
Yet I can sing you songs
You may want to hear,
Be a dear, help me find
More space, quiet, time,
Damn the roles
That rout my rhyme.

Sensate Armies Of The Shore

Mind presents no challenge
For the placid shore,
Its anxious thoughts, frantic pace,
Her precincts do deplore,
Mind rushes there to analyze,
To think and think some more,
Yet fails to wisely comprehend
What our short span is for,
Her baggage train is full and long
With past and future freighted,
Now with regret, now with fear,
She seldom is elated,
Her cooler's overstuffed with books,
Her beach time planned and set,
Her judgments and opinions
Mind's queenly coronet,
Yet quick as that mind is unhorsed,
Forced to leave the field,
Whene'er she settles on the beach,
And to the surf must yield,
Her much prized cogitation,
Her logic and her sense,
Evaporate like phantoms,
Submit to present tense,
The sensate armies of the shore
Chase all of mind away,
Draw back the weighty curtain,
Invite the soul to play.

Books Come First To Mind

When thinking of the Cape & Islands
Books come first to mind,
In treasured memories left behind,
Books, and the sacred places
They were kept until adopted, many gone now,
Mourned by a few with long memories,
Books you could touch, feel and treasure,
Used books, new books, compact Oxford editions,
Books from library sales, yard sales,
Estates of the bibliophiles,
Up and down the winding miles
That crisscross the conceptual Cape & Islands,
Thick paperbacks on the beaches,
Children's books that popped their colors,
Pulled you in, stories, tales, entrancing finds
That summoned summer's meandering minds,
Surfeited with beach and food,
Curious to see what each might find,

Pilgrimage places like the Yellow Umbrella,
The bright Brewster, cozy Mitchells on Main,
The bountiful Bunch of Grapes, the noble B&N,
Where The Sidewalk Ends,
Nantucket Bookworks, Tim's and Titcombs,
The gingerbread South Dennis Library,
The exquisite Brewster Ladies Library
And the musty, cluttered Parnassus,
Where Cagney still haunts the stacks

Head down, muttering in his distinctive voice,
While Vonnegut, Styron, and Mailer chat up
Ben Muse, the late, aptly named, stoic owner,

When thinking of the Cape & Islands
Books come first and last to mind,
Glorious, embraceable, tangible books,
Books you could hold like a lover,
Look here, another find!
Let's see what's there beneath her cover.

Castaway

Hide me here beneath your sky,
Far from the all-seeing eye
Of those in authority passing by,
Cover my tracks with your sands,
Instruct your waves heed my commands,
Sequester me behind a dune
Above which wandering shorebirds croon,
Place me far beyond the reach
Of those who mandate, those who preach,
Down along some lonesome beach,
Enshroud me deep within your fog,
Kettle pond, berried bog,
Help me vanish, let them say
He disappeared one diverting day,
Craved a place to hideaway,
To live at least one blameless day,
To breathe, to hear his glad heart say:
I flew the coop come what may,
Our wayward world so pressed me in,
I let my soul's deep life begin.

My Storied Cape

Friendships fade, parents pass,
Sibling bonds soon fray,
Though acquaintances may try,
You seldom make headway,
Lovers come, lovers go,
Leave lesions in the heart,
If infatuation comes
It plays no long-term part,
You make a home, then another,
Neighbors come and go,
Life appears to be all change,
Transition all you know,
Children nest, soon take flight,
Leave memories in their wake,
Is everything we count upon
The thing we must forsake?
Not all, I hear dear nature say,
Some things remain the same,
The pleasures of my storied Cape
Which you may yet reclaim.

Winter Do Your Worst

Winter do your worst this year,
With scowling skies, frigid blasts,
That last, and last, and last, and last,
Make your whiteout storms the norm,
Batter me and my fellows
With your furious, baleful bellows,
Your pitiless frost that settles in the bone,
Disdainful winds that commandeer the skies,
Howl about the house with menacing moan,
Driving us well indoors shivering and cursing,
And with your crusty, downy blanket of snow
Strangulate our stubbled fields and icy streams,
Unsettling all our dreams, as all the while we nurse
A secret dream of summer, whose glorious arrival
Will be even more welcome this year than last,
For in this life we cannot know good from bad,
Light from shade, until their polar opposite
From clear contrast is made,
Winter, do your worst this year and
Like a tedious, ill-mannered guest
Linger here well into tardy spring
When all your unrelenting scorn will bring
The best, most gratifying summer,
Measured against what came before,
When all our joy shall be the more.

Bliss To Borrow

To those of you who've suffered pain,
Whose wounds by callous word
Or deed yet remain,
Whose minds, all tangled,
Rout the joy within,
Whose days with errant,
Lonely thoughts begin,
Why hesitate to take my cure,
Comprised of endless skies,
Air so pure?

To those with spirits weighted down,
Upon whose face life paints a daily frown,
Who disregard my genial sun,
Whose psyche does from calm content
Too often run,
Why squander your days and
Forfeit nature's gift,
By giving my restoratives short shrift?
There is yet time to banish sorrow
And from my bounty bliss to borrow.

Anticipation

Looking forward to a trip
Seems such a pleasant thing,
You live in expectation
Of what time off will bring,
You win the trip and something more,
The joy of what you're hoping for,
Day by day, as it comes near,
Your mind is surfeited with cheer,
But don't be fooled, it's never smart
To look ahead and play the part
Of a dreamer,
If you do you'll lose the time
You spent anticipating,
Instead of living all those days
Now lost to contemplating, and
Having left the Now of then
And every single day of Zen,
When you finally hit the beach
You'll find it's well beyond your reach,
Since you don't live within the Now
You can't vacation anyhow,
Just leave vacations where they are
And never let the future spar
With the present.

Come My Children

Come my children, I said to my senses,
Let's have some wicked fun
Under a willing, welcoming sun,

Dear Touch you'll have a treat today,
Sand and water will give way
And what would you say
To the warmth of sun upon your skin?
Are you in?

Sweet Taste make haste
We're leaving soon,
Leave your belly full of room
For tasty clams, broiled fish,
Every other seafood dish,

Dearest Smell you seem unwell,
This day will your malaise dispel,
There are delightful airs about
You'll catch upon the wind no doubt,

And my lovely, lyrical Hearing,
So endearing,
What say you to a musical day?
The seashore's tuning far away
With drum rolls and a wavy beat,
An awesome, auditory treat,

Lastly, dear, insatiable Sight,
Today I trust you will delight,
As never you have heretofore
When next you gaze upon the shore,

Come my children,
This day we'll have some wicked fun,
I spy the slowly rising sun,
Be quick he has a mind to run.

Come To The Beach They Said

Come to the beach they said,
But I was resolute in my head,
Come to the shore they said,
But I would not be easily led,
Come for a swim they said
And off they sped,
While I remained a slugabed
Tucked in with my resentments,
Protected by revetments
Of stone, concrete, stainless steel
Where I could better feel my pain,
Nurture things far more germane
Than fun, and joy, and silly play,
When dear god it dawned on me,
I had misspent another day.

Come About

Come about sailor, slow your pace,
Trim your sails life's not a race,
Find a new heading,
Breathe slowly, slower still,
That's it, breathe again more deeply,
Be less ambitious, stop striving, efforting,
Proving yourself to yourself, to others,
Contending, running always and ever
Before the wind, drop the desperation,
The restless doing and going,
The frenzied thinking and planning,
The constant movement,
The running away from yourself
And the things that matter,
Change your tack, just be for a time,
Stage a mutiny, toss
Your autocratic mind in the brig,
Move through the wind
To a more worthy heading
That will reveal what you were born to:
An untroubled spirit, a contented mind,
A noble heart and
This achingly beautiful shoreline,
Border of your first terrestrial home,
Come about sailor,
There's time enough to roam.

Sweet Summer On The Cape

Why is sunny weather
Inclined to summon joy?
Why should rays of sunshine
Content more easily deploy,
Than chill, low and cloudy skies
Which when they meet the mind and eyes
Just as swiftly do destroy
The mood the late, bright sun did buoy?
Why should balmy, temperate, mild,
Summon up the carefree child,
While cold, dark, gunmetal gray,
Leaves every mind in disarray?
Why should months of snow and sleet
High hopes and fortitude deplete,
While warmth and sun will seldom fail
To offer up the Holy Grail?
Yet there's a place not far from here
One may one's soul reshape,
Where winsome weather is the rule,
Sweet summer on the Cape.

Look For Me On Sunset Hill

If I am gone and with a will
In search of summer's treasure trove,
Look for me on Sunset Hill,
Wrinkle Point, or Ryder's Cove,
If White Cedar Swamp looks fair,
I may be denning deep in there,
Perhaps I've gone to Cuttyhunk
Or lovely Lackeys Bay,
Sheepfold Hill or Scrabble Town
For each is far away,
I may be found at Fiddler Cove,
Bells Neck or Basset Isle,
Or sailing out of Wychmere
To linger for a while
On the Sound,
I might haunt the Hill of Storms,
Cold Harbor, Barley Neck,
Or may be off of Schooner Bar
Reclining on a deck,
I may have sailed from Sesuit,
As far as Sandy Neck,
Or diving off of Eastham
Surveying some old wreck,
Perhaps I've hiked old Lookout Hill,
Sailed cross Dogfish Bar,
Lost myself in Skunknet Woods

Or wandered off by car
Along the King's Highway or
Some other charming byway,
On second thought don't look for me
If I am gone and by the sea.

Conspiracy

The shrewd sun is a plotter,
The secretive sea a schemer,
The conniving breeze
Their confederate,
All co-conspirators,
All determined
To undermine the mind,
Overpower thought,
Rout worry and fear
As long as you are near,

The stealthy sun is an intriguer,
The vast ocean a colluder,
The wily wind a deluder,
The powdery sand an intruder,
And when they join forces
Against you in full battle array,
I'm very sure there is no cure
And that you will be vanquished.

All Embracing Soulful Sea

Something more than this cold city,
Something well proportioned, pretty,
Something for the soul to breathe,
Give the frantic mind reprieve,
Something not so narrowed in
With glass and steel and corporate sin,
Something if I might conjecture,
Lacking ego architecture,
Something elemental, true,
Where shadows won't obscure the view,
Something far less insincere
Where I might shed the figment fear,
Something to enhance romance,
Give the heart a decent chance,
Someplace that will slow my pace,
Soul instead of mind embrace,
Something life designed for me,
The all-embracing, soulful sea.

First Ocean Swim

All winter long, springtime too,
I hungered much like you
For an open ocean swim,
Full of vigor, full of vim,
I thought to capture sky blue bliss
And so dismiss one early dawn
The urban accretions laid thick upon
My pale, dry skin,
And so begin my happy time,
Free from snow, relentless rime,

I longed to hurtle high and far,
With the billowing breakers spar,
Splash and frolic unobserved
Till all offseason dreams are served,
I craved to traipse her tip-top dunes,
Translate her driftwood runes,
Put a glow on pale, white skin,
Let the timeless tide soak in,
I dreamt of merging with the sea
To feel how lovely life could be.

Born In Stealth

Born in stealth from a haggard heart
She blossoms in the mind,
Giving my day a benevolent start,
Do I leave all duty behind?
A single thought, inchoate wish,
Brightens my heavy soul,
Do I dare take this day
Forsaking every role,
All daily imperatives?
Come to me I hear her say,
Lay down your woe and care,
What's a single merry day
But respite from despair?
But, I say, I won't, I can't,
My duties call to me,
My kids, my dog, the boss, the house,
They'll never let me be,
Emboldened now, more urgent still,
She whispers in my ear,
The boss is home, the kids at school,
What is there left to fear?
In quick retreat my conscience yields,
Little left to say,
I call in sick, cruise the coast,
While away the day,
To a heavy heart she comes in stealth,
Seduces before the dawn,
She the mistress of mental health,
You the woebegone.

The Beach Is But A Looking Glass

The beach is but a looking glass
That mirrors what it finds,
It holds our own thoughts up to us,
Reflects what's in our minds,
It's neutral and unbiased,
Unlike our probing shrinks,
Does not project, throw back on you
What its unconscious thinks,
It has no separate point of view,
No feeling overlay,
It leaves you free to listen to
The things your mind will say,
So come on down, spend a day,
No fuss, no couch, no pay,
Far more fetching than your shrink,
Unwise to delay.

Midyear Metamorphosis

To prepare for summer
I transition from mind to spirit,
From declaiming to listening,
Doing to being, man to nature,
Confronting to yielding, self to others,
Distraction to mindfulness,
Agitation to quietude, and
Remind myself that I am not alone
In this midyear transformation of the soul,
For the innate peace, peerless patience,
And incomparable beauties of the coast
Will gentle me along,
Seduce me with their song.

Liniments Of The Littoral

The emollient of a beach day
Trumps the emolument of a work day,
Beach balm beats bonus and
I now put the onus on you to disagree
For nearly all concur with me,
Sea salve surpasses salary,

I have an early morning notion
To apply her liquid lotion
On this moody Monday,
To moisturize, revitalize,
Conceal myself from auditing eyes.

Cape & Islands Cri De Coeur

Keep sunless cities your touted towers,
Cries she with fish and chips,
Send me your anxious, your oppressed,
Your corporate hordes longing to be free,
The joyless jetsam of your soulless canyons,
Deliver these, the ambition-tossed, to me,
I lift my sun beside the shimmering sea.

The Canal

No one can touch you once you're across,
No one may lay a hand,
No creditor, stranger, peevish boss,
You've reached the Promised Land,
Regardless of how you made your escape,
Via car, plane, or boat,
Once you've crossed the Cape Cod Canal
You'll have so many reasons to gloat,

This celestial channel, singular strait,
Marks the boundary 'tween heaven and earth,
Beyond which you're unassailable
As you transit from sadness to mirth,
No one can wound you once you're across,
Not a soul can lay a hand,
No worries, fears or bellicose boss,
May intrude on the Promised Land.

Here in New England

Here in New England
We keep our bodies under wraps,
After youth and its grand play
We tend to keep them hid away,
We weigh them down with woolly coats,
Constrict their range of motion,
Till summer gives hard won consent
To greater locomotion,

In summertime we greet the sun
And the bodies we inhabit,
Yet when the summer season's run
We imitate the rabbit,
Go underground once more,

What is it by the sea and shore
That liberates our flesh?
That does the pinched
New England soul
So lovingly refresh?

Dolce Far Niente

Like a true New Englander
I resolved to use my beach vacation
In a prudent and productive manner
To achieve the following:
Master the mind, heal the heart,
Cease to be a man apart,
Improve my intellect through reading,
Stalled career through more succeeding,
Tighten spending, curb condescending,
Write a book, conceive a play,
Make the most of every day,
Learn to play the cello,
Become an amiable fellow,
Paint the house, lay a walk,
Learn more jargon, talk the talk,
Learn to make béarnaise,
Master turn of phrase,
Strive to be more humble,
Jettison both whine and grumble,
Then I thought of Italy,
Everyone's first choice
If we could visit anywhere,
Give travel dreams a voice,
No longer do I plan to spend
A single minute more,
All self-improvement did suspend
Then headed for the shore,
With not a single goal in mind
Save joy and nothing more.

Actives & Contemplatives

How nice of you to welcome
Both actives and contemplatives,
Bravely placing them side by side
With each receding, ebbing tide,
Actives flinging flying discs,
Running with their kites,
Contemplatives with their tiny chairs
Immersed in book delights,
College boys with footballs
Shouting as they run,
Scholars with their weighty tomes
Averse to having fun,
Those who wrestle with the breeze
To save the daily news,
Those who'd rather laugh and swim
Than world events peruse,
Those who welcome all your world
With action, fun and play,
Those immured in their own thoughts
Who keep your world at bay,
How nice of you to welcome,
How kind of you to serve,
Those who would embrace your world,
Those who would observe.

Like Pancakes On A Griddle

Midday air humid and thick
Yet most welcome
After our interminable winter,
Whose chill, bony hands
Reached too far into early spring,
Multitudes lie here today,
Depleted, motionless,
Face down like war wounded,
Inert, enervated,
All along the beachfront,
Greedily sucking up high heat,
Pale, vulnerable flesh blushing red,
Morphing to a dark chocolate,
The only movement
The occasional wriggling
Of reddened, peeling toes,
The only sound, a low,
Murmuring moan
As ponderous limbs prepared
For the next slow, searing turn
Of innumerable, lifeless bodies,
Groaning, grunting, marinating,
Sizzling multitudes lie here,
Like pancakes on a griddle.

Behold Your Town

Most fortunate dwellers,
Happy habitants,
Satisfied settlers,
Royal residers here,
Of all places far or near,
On this Cape,
These Islands,
Full-favored of Providence,
Best loved of the gods,
To breathe its ocean air,
Daily greet its sun,
When your span of life
Might well have run
In another time or place,
Surely blessed of all your race,
Consider:
Not the city, nor the wild,
No safer place to raise a child,
Right amount of people,
Mix of secular and steeple,
Four full seasons,
Flurries, gentle rain,
Hills low enough to tame,
Safe from fetid, urban air
Limpid lakes, salt marsh to spare,
Orchards weighted down
With fruit,
Creatures here
From deer to newt,

Trees of every form and size,
Bright blooms enough
To please all eyes,
Varied landscapes all around,
Serenest nights
Without a sound,
Long days of peace,
No drums of war,
No martial tunes
Need you deplore,
Heroes resting in your soil,
Balanced mix of fun and toil,
Easy blend of age and race,
No frantic, anxious city pace,
Unpretentious, often humble,
No geographic cause
To grumble,
Thank your stars, your fate,
Your luck and have no truck
With those who whine,
Who for other coastlines pine,
No cause to frown,
Behold your town.

Feeling Free

Here I feel free
To show some skin
Or not,
To hit what I had overshot,
Play the dauntless aquanaut,
Mimic crab or guillemot,
Crawl inside a lobster pot
Or not,

Here I feel free
To tan upon this beauty spot,
So smooth, so soft, so piping hot,
To sip some brandy, apricot,
Make myself a microdot,
Veg out or play the pepperpot
Or not,

Here I feel free,
To recoup what inner child forgot,
Untie every Windsor knot,
Play Jason or an Argonaut,
Boost my glow to megawatt,
Give my soul a booster shot
Or not,

Here I feel free,
Free to be me,
Instead of the me
You'd like me to be.

High Head To Nauset

When long awaited summer with its warming rays
Gentled us all with ever lengthening days,
And revivified creatures, long hidden in the chilly deep,
Made summer frolic, joyous leap,
And soothing breezes swayed sea grass,
And bathers of all shapes did pass
The slowing time of day,
And lazy, lax, idle intent held sway,
And graceful shorebirds swooped and soared
With envied, avian esprit de corps,
And small blue crabs did sideways walk
Beneath the squawking gull and hawk,
And the Cape's raised arm called to all
To rise and come with the reach
Of each and every powdery beach
Along its gorgeous ocean flanks,
Then did I most eagerly join ranks
With random walkers giving thanks,
That our trek to Nauset Beach from High Head
Had roused us from loitering in our beds,
And all, in unison, praised with unalloyed elation
Our kindest Lord of all creation,
So there, below the imposing dunes of Province Lands,
Obeying all of His celestial commands,
We commenced our Holy Expedition,
Fervently hoping thereby to avoid perdition
And its scary, scalding, searing roast,
So of my pleasant comrades let me now boast:
There was a Lifeguard, sinewy and lean,

Full of duty, chaste and clean,
Who vowed to rescue, swim and save
All those tossed on wild and wicked wave,
There was a Mermaid, lithe, supple, far too sweet,
With shimmering scales from waist to feet,
Who gracefully swam her way along,
Humming a haunting siren song,
A prickly Pirate joined our group,
Just in that day from Guadeloupe,
Grizzled, whiskered, gruff voiced with missing teeth,
Two pistols and bejeweled knife in sheathe,
And a woeful Wraith there was from a schooner lost,
Whom every bather she did accost
With pleas to find her next of kin,
Her spectral limbs all paper thin,
A Pilgrim too, foreign born,
Who gorged himself on pilfered corn,
Then luckily found a gurgling spring
For little life enhancing water did we bring,
And a Balding Man of shiny pate
With leering eyes who joined us late,
Who shamed and shocked our saintly prudes
While ogling sunbathing nudes,
A Minister too, full of pious prayer,
Whose ready flock were the fishers there,
Who easily rescued with fervent beseeching
All rowdy sailors through his preaching
From falling into the abyss of sin,
So our dearest Lord might let them in,

A Wild Baby too, without a stich,
From scorching rays now black as pitch,
An impulsive, adorable, bouncing boy,
Who laughed and played and gleefully sang,
Most happily led our seaside gang,
A high-minded, reflective Author there also was,
A nonconforming intellect who caused a buzz,
Who hailed, they said, from Concord Town,
Whose transcendent thoughts formed a frown,
An Oceanographer too was there
With manner somewhat doctrinaire,
Who knew the ways of fish and fowl,
Who shamefully walked without a towel,
And a lonely, loquacious Retiree
Whose tone though sad was full of sincerity,
Whose loving memory of his wife
Conveyed his joy of married life,
And sundry others on the way,
Each of them with much to say,
Who all regaled our close-knit throng
With tales of laughing gulls and song,
We stepped off as the rising sun
Commenced its mandatory run,
Filled with bliss we said a prayer
For all our motley gathered there,
And as our pilgrimage did begin
We sang a melodious, well-known hymn,
Then sweet Wild Baby took the lead
And to his wise and sweet commands
Our pious troupe did then accede.

Leave Us

Knees buckle, the breath catches,
The brain can't hold a thought,
Expectation floods the soul,
Five keen senses wait
Like impatient gluttons
On a sensory feast,
The agitated blood rushes to every
Extremity, while the stomach lurches,
Tightens and churns,
Those clever twins of language,
Words and wit,
Desert their tongue-tied host and
Poise and felicitous expression
In quick succession
Join them in permanent, linguistic exile,
Faintheartedness, long a stranger,
Now makes a home where courage
And fortitude once dwelt,
I struggle to speak and a stammer of falsettos
And high C's exit the mouth, normal words
Stumble, chaotically collide in a vain attempt
At sound and sense,
These and more, my friends,
Are the symptoms of love
Awakened in me once again come summer,
When first I catch sight of her
Captivating curves, her soft, seductive, sandy flanks,
Breathe in her seaside scents and happily surrender
To the intoxicating rhythms of her ambient music,
Leave us.

Maketh Tame The Waves

Please place the raucous over there,
Dear Lord hear my prayer,
Maketh tuneful their musical taste,
Lord hear my prayer,
Secureth my brelly against the breeze,
Lord hear my prayer,
Tempereth the scorching heat of day,
Lord hear my prayer,
Make the sun to shineth all the day,
Lord hear my prayer,
Maketh bearable the proximate
Lamentations of babes,
Lord hear my prayer,
Safeguard my things while I wadeth,
Lord hear my prayer,
Scattereth the gathering clouds,
Lord hear my prayer,
Remind me to applyeth sunscreen,
Lord hear my prayer,
Watch over me while I swimeth,
Lord hear my prayer,
Maketh tame the waves,
Lord hear my prayer.

Action

Quiet on the set please,
Cue Beaming Sun Child,
Up the sky blue stairway son, slower please,
Much slower, facing forward, thank you,
Lower Pale Moon Child,
Mute morning colors, softer,
Cumulus Cloud Attendants now please,
Not too near Beaming Sun Child,
Space yourselves out,
Cue Flapping Shorebirds,
Light on your toes please,
Stage left, stage right,
Synchronizing release, now flyaway all,
Melodious sounds please,
Pianissimo rising to crescendo,
Low wave shushing sounds,
Muted Gull cries,
Soft breeze wind machines on low,
Waking Beige Sand Children, rising slowly,
To standing positions,
Arms interlocked, good, good,
Turning in unison to face Beaming Sun Child,
Turntable Mermaids now please, stage right,
Full smiles everyone, waving emerald tails,
Cue Shell Children, chased playfully
By clattering Crab Toddlers with pincers,
Sforzando please, as Three Great White Toddlers
Emerge from trap door center stage,
Beige Sand Children now scatter, watch your step,

That's a wrap, brilliant, rehearsal tomorrow,
Every day thereafter till fall,
Thanks all, same time,
Ta-ta.

Joy

I'm thrilled to be alive today, irrepressibly,
Ecstatically, unapologetically happy,
Oh say can you see happy, here on this Cape,
These Islands, and I shall be demonstrative
And most compelling in making that clear to you,
I shall linger long on my favorite bayside beach,
Be prudent in pursuit of an attractive tan,
Devour tasty seafood, soft serve cones,
Swim into, around and through her turquoise waters,
Walk hand in hand along her amber sands
With the one I am devoted to
Whose reciprocal devotion exceeds my own,
I shall reacquaint myself with puerile play and
Nurturing, nautical nature, celebrate the
Intense beauty circumnavigating my soul here,
I will see the best in my fellows,
Make allowances for them in all cases,
Employ and delight in my five senses,
Embody a deep gratitude
For this coastal horn of plenty,
Add to my store of fond memories,
And swell with gladness to the widest,
Salty margins of this peerless place,
Every swift second
Of every vanishing minute.

List O List

List, O list, to the sounds of the shore,
List to the song of the sand,
List, O list, to the deep ocean's roar,
Akin to a marching band,

List, O list, to the sonorous surf,
The mellifluous melodies here,
List, O list, to the tidal tunes,
Come closer and you will hear,

List, O list, to the harmonies
Of the clouds, the winds, and the sky,
List, O list, to the euphonies
Of the bathers and passersby,

List, O list, to the concord within,
Subtle strains of a heart now at rest,
List, O list, to the chant of a soul,
Blithe spirit no longer repressed.

Asleep By The Shore

Beneath the shade of a broad oak tree,
Not thinking too hard of what he might be,
Our singer who never opened his eyes
Lingered and languished under changeable skies,

Singer awake, open the seam,
Capture our meaning, make sense of our dream,

We spotted him beachcombing, bathing and such,
Feared he might never convey very much,
The world spun around, broke every heart,
While the singer like us never made a true start,

Singer awake, write of our dream,
Capture our meaning, find us a theme,

Asleep by the shore, seduced by the breeze,
He did what he wanted, did what he pleased,
Dream catchers were left by his somnolent side,
In the hope he and his muse would no longer hide,

Singer arise, don't sleep though our dream,
Capture our lives, things aren't what they seem,

They say he's been sighted high up on a hill,
Awake to his duty, in touch with his will,
Netting his monarchs, blue sulphurs too,
Sending us dreamers his bright billet-doux.

A Kind Of Portal

All things open up here, widen, enlarge,
Not only the sky, the horizon, the view,
The breadth of comprehension too is new,
The cramped soul hears the summons of nature,
Expands, fills the space, uncoils,
And like the pretty petals of a waking flower
In slow motion compliantly opens,
The narrow corridors of the mind
Find breathing room,
The hesitant heart unclutches,
Possibilities multiply, certainties loosen,
Dear defenses are dropped
And the weighty baggage of emotion
Is swiftly unpacked,

Why should the shore cause such things to be,
With only sand, sky, and sea
To work its magic with?
Why should the shore right the soul?
Course correct the mind and heart?
I suspect it is a kind of portal
For every weary mortal
To see through to the very heart of things,
To apprehend the essentials
That cause the irrepressible soul to dance
To the beat-keeping waves
Under a hand-clapping sun.

Enchantress

I tumble down the dunes that yield
To show the wonders they concealed,
Across her ecru sands I run
To greet her in the morning sun,
Along her windswept flanks I fly
To see her preen beneath the sky,
I spy her new-formed sheen of shells,
Sea crockery left by gentle swells,
I feel her winds across my face,
Quicken now my lagging pace,
I gulp her pure, unsullied air,
Joyful now, without a care,
Then splash against her chilly feet,
For this is how we always meet,
I hurl myself upon her breast,
Dive to seek the treasure chest
Of the hidden, cooling plumes
That deep beneath her surface bloom,
Then swim below the cresting waves,
My inamorata saves for me alone,
Like a dolphin, splash and play,
Ask her how she is today.

I Am The Catalyst

I am the catalyst, I am the shore,
You may come and silent be
Or deeper thoughts explore,
I will aid your silence,
Cleanse your brain of thought,
Or will abet a deeper dive,
Help loose the mind made knot,
How you visit's up to you,
I'll not direct your soul,
Except to caution now and then
Tranquility's your goal,
I am the healer, I am the sea,
I'll work with what you bring to me.

And Songs To Sing

Who formed these creatures of the shore?
Gave them eyes, brains, so much more?
Who gave them claws, feathered wing,
And songs to sing, the ones who do?
Does randomness make sense to you?
Who gave them all their shapes and size?
Fins and feathers, piercing cries?
Who formed each for their own domain,
Along this shore in sun and rain?
Who conceived their varied parts?
Who mastered all of nature's arts?
Some say these creatures came to be
Without intent like you and me,
Yet I, like you, have questions still,
It all suggests a hidden will.

Doctor Cape & Doctor Islands

How are you feeling?
Mind still reeling?
Not any more,
Is it the shore?
(They laugh knowingly),
Negative thoughts?
No shoulds or oughts
If that's what you mean,
Anxiety, fear?
All crystal clear,
Sleeping well?
Can't you tell?
Enhanced esteem?
With this vanishing cream?
(Displays sunblock),
Come tell us more,
We seem to have
Such fine rapport.

Dawn At CBI

Just north of Chatham Light she lies,
Softly serenaded by the gaping moon
Who, full and low over the dark sea,
To her nightly loves to croon
And be a subtle competitor
To the garish sun who
In early morn brashly thrusts
His searing, golden eye
Into her sea-fronting glass,
Illuminates the mercurial sandbars
To sparkle, shift and shimmer,
Rouses the lazy, lumbering seals
And into the shark-infested sea
Instills a deadly glimmer,
Floods the raised forearm of the Cape
With heartening warmth and light,
Wakes the nimble, little, rainbow fleet,
Long at anchor to shake off night
And put to sea,
Calls to you and to me to rise,
Acknowledge with our jaded eyes
Her rarefied beauty,
Alluring, well-made, stately,
Full in love with nature
With whom she dwells,
Sand, sky and sea, its azure swells,
Our seacoast nonpareil,
That neither words nor melodious rhyme
Her timeless beauties fairly tell.

First Beach Walk

My first beach walk
On hallowed ground
Blessed with loss of weight,
Something I had not foreseen,
Did not anticipate,

First to fall was career,
Face planting on the sand,
Then regrets and all my debts
In one wrack line did land,

Then my fears did disappear,
From my soul were banished,
It seemed as though my extra pounds
Had somehow simply vanished,

No longer will I strive to lose
To get myself in shape,
In one fell swoop I'll shed those pounds
First beach walk on the Cape.

A Blue Gray Wading Bird

A blue-gray wading
Bird
Came up the golden sand and
Decked out in plumage fine,
Explained to me while
Foraging free and
Going down the line of a salt marsh, that
He'd spied a melancholy mermaid and
Intent to free her sea-green hair
Just now entangled in a net and
Knowing well if he had let her
Lie,
Maybe she would sooner die and
Never join her merman love waiting
On the
Pier above,
Queer, I thought, this bird should come,
Request from me, an old beach bum,
Some help to free a
Tangled maid
Undone by netting overlaid, yet
Verily I say to you
We went and made her good as new,
Xplaining just as best we could
Y now she should, bereft of fear, with
Zealous pace regain the pier.

A Fluttering Of Umbrellas

A brotherhood of barnacles,
A synod of sun worshipers,
A posse of parking attendants,
A luminescence of lighthouses,
A lamentation of cloud cover,
A jutting of jetties,
A blubbering of seals,
A pride of CEO's,
A sorority of shorebirds,
A casting of fishers,
An exultation of moods,
A mustering of mariners,
A gathering of gulls,
A protrusion of paunch,
A constellation of starfish,
A crenellation of sandcastles,
A cornucopia of coolers,
A swarm of sunbathers,
A cluster of clams,
A vexation of greenheads,
A riot of colors,
A proliferation of sunshine,
A society of skimmers,
A corps of cormorants,
A torment of tunes,
A tumult of teens,
A protectorate of lifeguards,
A coterie of cockleshells,
An exhibition of flesh,

A benevolence of breezes,
An amalgamation of algae,
A welter of wildflowers,
A jubilation of swimmers,
A declination of dunes,
An assignation of lovers,
A bevy of beach roses,
A profusion of plankton,
A breach of whales and
A fluttering of umbrellas.

Carried On The Breeze

I set the bar too high and knew it,
One week only, to reclaim joy,
Tame the overbearing mind,
All cognitive clutter leave behind,
Yet when I first caught sight of this beach,
The secluded cove beyond,
First heard, sweetly carried on the breeze,
The enchanting, high-pitched voices
Of unseen, elfin children just beyond the dune,
I knew I had a decent chance,
Though I had set the bar too high
And knew it.

This Coast Is Full Of Music

This coast is full of music
For those attuned to hear,
Symphonic variations
For the highly sensitive ear,

Things that are blown or blow:
Like wind and breeze, nautical flags,
Blowholes of whales, flapping sails,
Beach umbrellas, foghorns, birdsong
And the songs of little children,

Things that bang, percussive things:
Like crashing waves, clanging rigging,
Flukes on the sea, booms of thunder,
Crab claw and bivalve castanets,
Caught fish wriggling and flapping,
Oars and paddles on the water,
Seals splashing and fireworks,

Strings and things you scrape across:
Like pebbles tumbling in the tide,
Boats nudging their docks,
Mermaids using their long, green locks
As lyres, and seals strumming whiskers,

This coast is full of music,
Euphonious, atonal,
Metallic and sublime,
Symphonic variations
For those who take the time
To listen, with imagination.

What Can A Beach Teach

For one thing, flow,
As in and out she goes,
Patience too,
The spirit's wise delay
Foreign to me and to you,
And kindness
For she gently welcomes all,
The plump, the thin,
The short, the tall,
Integrity as well
Reflected in her rhythmic swells,
And conviviality
With her open-hearted span,
Salty arms outstretched to man,
And at her best a chance to rest,
To find solitude and inner peace,
A quiet corner for the frenzied soul,
Anodyne to make one whole.

What Shall I Call You Friend

What shall I call you friend?
What name do you go by?
"Shore" is less common,
More formal, poetical even,
And with "the" as antecedent
Lends you a significance well deserved,
While "coast" suggests elongation,
Distance from me to you on land
Or from the water looking back at your
Long, low, littoral profile,
Or from the air as you precisely mark
Your intricate boundary with the land,
"Strand" seems a bit too grand,
August and imperial, yet unlike the others
Literally embodies your sandy essence,
"Sea" suggests vision,
Propagation over a wide area,
And you are a vision
With impressive depth and majesty,
Mystery and romance,
"Ocean" calls to mind potency,
Fathomless, blue depths,
Primal beingness, first causes
And the shy, submerged gods behind
Your gorgeous mask,
Or might you prefer the simpler "beach"
Which summons thoughts of ease,
Time away, swatches of color,

A marvelous multiplicity of sensations,
Distilled joys and the sensual warmth
Of a brightly beaming sun?
What shall I call you friend?
What name do you go by?

A Little God Of The Sea

I saw a babe upon the sand,
The churning sea did he command,
Naked, plopped at water's edge,
This tale is true and not alleged,
He gurgled, giggled, slapped at waves,
Mocking each as watery knaves,
Into wavelets he would lean,
Quick disappear then pop up clean
To slap the quiet space between,
Daring another roller to come
And toss him off his ample bum,
He seemed a little god of the sea,
Unselfconscious, happy, free,
Oblivious to others on the sand
Who neither waves nor winds command,
With each new wave his joy increased,
He summoned more without surcease,
Then wishing for myself his rapture,
I too plopped down and sought to capture
The same,
Yet when the next wild wavelet came
I did not laugh or shout with glee
Or behave unselfconsciously,
Perhaps afraid someone might see?
I spied a babe upon the sand,
Each marching wave he did command,
Though I tried, I still could not,
What might it be that I've forgot?

Mantle Of Beauty

No one is deceived for long
By the mantle of beauty
The shore drapes over itself
All along this coastal shelf,
No matter the ferocity of storm or gale,
Plaintive cry of fish or whale,
Undersea combat of predator and prey,
Shellfish hungry birds waylay,
Flotsam, jetsam on the beach or
Flailing swimmers out of reach,
No matter the turbulence of sky and sea,
It yet remains miraculous to me
How the shore such chaos hides,
As over all she gently slides
Her mantle of beauty.

First Day

I see the dune, spy the beach,
Time to clear the mind,
Achieve that state of consciousness
That leaves all thought behind,
I grasp the rope, climb the dune,
Soon reach its rounded crest,
Take one life-affirming breath,
Set my brain at rest,
I notice all the bathers
Staring up at me,
Waiting to size my body up,
Nadir to apogee,
My mind intrudes once again,
I hesitate and think,
Am I taut and trim enough
Here now on the brink?
Did I exercise enough?
Is this the perfect suit?
Have bye-bye muscles
Come back home,
Lost cellulite to boot?
Should I have passed
On cheese and fries,
Glazed donuts, beer, and chips?
If I had would I be pleased
With bottom, legs and hips?
Should I have jogged a million miles?
Passed on heavy cream?
Summer peace in ruins now,

At risk my self-esteem,
Then a thought occurred to me,
They're wondering the same,
I tell my mind to take a hike,
Like them so pleased I came.

Lamberts Cove Beach

Let the ambitious win the world,
I am content right here,
Letting my heart find its home
Where surf and sand are near,
I sense their anxious seeking,
Daily deep unease,
They make me nervous, every one,
Whom ego strive to please,
I cannot change their natures,
Turn their minds around,
Nor can I fill their empty space
Or drag to lost and found,
Yet I can rescue one lone soul
Well within my reach and
Find the solace others crave
Here upon this beach.

Savor The Sea

Savor the sea, salute her salty majesty,
Anchor your spirit in her nourishing depths,
Create a sea rapport and more,
Discourse with her, drench your soul in her,
Let her lay siege to you,
Orchestrate your feelings and
Inspire mirth and contentment,
Permit her to replenish you and knit up
The frayed ends of your life,
Reciprocate her gifts with gifts of your own,
Swaddle your spirit in her benefactions,
Dance a quadrille on her sacred sands,
Replenish your long depleted stores
With her selflessness and bounty,
Reconcile yourself to her soothing rhythms,
Her ceaseless movement and
With amazement and unwonted gratitude
Receive it all with a solemn silence.

Are You Brave

Then sleep alone upon this beach,
No other voice or hand in reach,
No other soul to fend off things
Night and sea and darkness bring,
Are you bold?
Then lie upon this sand death cold,
Under a slice of menacing moon,
Beneath the now indifferent stars,
Upon a strand whose pitch now mars
What hours ago was yours and ours,
Are you intrepid?
Let the cloak of night drape over you,
Notice now your lost composure,
Your sudden, startling vulnerability,
Your nascent sense of dread
That makes a home within your head,
Notice too the lighthouse sweep
Across the dark and murky deep,
Aren't you one with the universe?
Then why should feelings so perverse
Clutch your heart, torment your mind?
Or will you find
The universe is much like you
Comprised of joy and terror too?
You will not lie, nor will you sleep,
Nor confront the scary deep,
Nor will you stand your ground tonight,

All alone so full of fright,
If I were you I'd leave this place,
And from your trembling heart erase
This horrid thing you cannot name,
And yet we both know why you came.

Sunrise Service

This coast is my cathedral,
Its sands my local church,
This fissured dune my chapel
No devil may besmirch,
Its shorebirds are my choristers,
Sea creatures are the flock,
The vaulted sky that holds us in
Impels my soul take stock,
Her tidal flats comprise the nave,
Her depths the sacristy,
Cumulus clouds her buttresses,
A fitting place for me,
Her spires pierce the open sky
With columns of cobalt blue
And every soul that suns itself
Reclines within a pew,
Till windows made of sea glass,
Lit by the setting sun,
Tell to each communicant
When daily worship's done,
I would not trade this sacred space
For brick or stone or wood,
Where man first saw the face of god,
When on the shore she stood.

Outside Shower

Few things here are more sublime
Than an outside shower,
A simple, sensual, glorious gift
From a caring, higher power,
Dotting the landscape,
Appended to a rental,
Nothing about them incidental,
Some are hidden from voyeur's eyes,
Some slats will give the prudes surprise,
Some are gleaming, all fenced in,
Most wide enough to set foot in,
My own is old, very rusted,
Its nozzle sad, sea salt encrusted,
Yet when I strip beneath the sun,
Lock its stockade door,
I realize then as I had not
Just what a shower's for,
It's then my soul takes sudden flight
Borne upon sea breeze,
Though you may spy a bit of skin
My goal is not to tease,
Too few praise what I extol,
What lifts my heavy heart and soul,
What does my weary flesh console.

On The Swan River

Where was I before I landed?
Am I found? am I stranded?
What is this encases me?
These arms, these legs,
Blue orbs that see?
Did a soul climb inside,
Make a home, hitch a ride,
Till devouring death
Reclaims the breath?
Or am I and my body one
Beneath this glow of setting sun?
Why this world so round and blue?
Why one short life then we're through?
Why put here my love to find,
Whose hand I take, soon leave behind?
Lots of questions, few replies,
Many queries, much surmise,
Why surrounded so by space?
Alone or members of a scattered race?
Why don't you agree with me
Who seem to see reality so differently?
How odd we go about our day,
Never stop to say what's up?
If we're unconscious, sound asleep,
What better way to secrets keep?
Still it all appears quite odd
If we are children of a god.

Chatham Bars Inn

If you're not in love
When you come
You will be when you go,
With someone new and her,
And nature's magisterial show,
She gifts with deep sleeps,
Soporific night air,
Panoramic views and sugared sand,
Yet do not take her hand
Until she offers it,
In a day or two you will be drunk
With joy and ease
For she truly seeks to please,
Yet know this, gentle guest,
Though most welcome and
You'll find here much of home,
She lies here to be near
Her first love the sea
In all his coastal majesty,
Nor will she wound her love
Or make him over jealous
Though ever zealous with you
To flirt and seduce,
It is no use, she is taken,
Through all her regal years,
All her sun-kissed, sovereign days,
She will not turn her longing gaze
To you or to me
From her betrothed the sea.

Corporation Beach
From Snack Bar Hill

Come see the this beach the way the gods see it,
Slightly removed and above, as if peering
Curiously over a cloud,
Your amazed eyes and muted tongue
Capturing her unblemished shoreline
In one admiring, non-judgmental glance,
A living, stirring, wriggling crescent
Resplendent with color and movement,
Full of chatter and all the innocent fun
Humans can pack into one blessed bit of coast,
Where all ages, sizes, voices,
Modes of dress and shapes
Appear to have reached a miraculous, summer truce,
Now tan together in a marvel of harmony
And cramped neighborliness,
A buoyant horde of revelers worshiping the sun,
Venerating the sea, playing at the edge
Of the beautiful bay in conspicuous, sensual proximity,
Convincingly pretending there are no strangers,
Only unmet friends,
Come see this beach from snack bar hill,
The elevated, innocent domain
Of parents and children,
Feel for a fleeting moment
The rapture of your life,
And the incomparable, dazzling beauty
Of the creation you were meant to share
For a time.

Denizen

Darkling dweller in the deep,
Whose lurking presence
Will forever keep
Me vigilant
When I sail, when I swim,
When I think of the dim,
Unlit, rayless depths
That house you deep within,
Indistinct inhabitant of the sea,
Remorseless resident, cold cousin,
Are you far this day or near to me?
This water is warm, this day is bright,
Will you bring a touch of night?
Was that pinch of crab a sign?
Do you have intent to dine
On me?

In Medias Res

I come to the Cape & Islands
Down on our species,
Two thumbs down, Dante down,
Fed up with meanness, wars, insincerities,
Vulgarities, manipulations, inauthenticity,
Half-truths and blinkered minds,
Starved for a de minimis sign of integrity,
Railing at our half-finished, snails-paced evolution,

Yet after two blissful weeks
I head home reassured, feeling blessed
To be counted a fortunate member
Of such a noble human race,
Now seeing pervasive woundedness
Where before I had surmised nefarious intent,
Now assuming the best of motivations,
Imagining their troubles, poor luck in life,
Projecting goodness on everyone,
Cutting the whole world slack,

I now see that my beginning and my end
Were both misguided and extreme,
That my fellow vacationers
Are most fairly assessed,
Most objectively indicted and redeemed
Precisely in the middle of my two week vacation,
During that second Saturday, round midday,
Just after my categorical condemnation,
Just before my blanket absolution.

If You Should See Me On The Beach

Be careful how you speak to me, like you I am a mess,
A mix of great uncertainties I here to you confess,
A jumble of emotions, blend of light and dark,
Some devils food, some angel cake, from one celestial spark,
At times so deeply centered, at others blown apart,
A slave of deep emotion, faithful footman to my heart,
Dupe of mind-made thoughts and acts who sometimes gets it right,
My skipping, sunny, summer days quick followed by dark night,
Encased within a body, imprisoned just like you,
I came without a history, now seek the god's broad view,
Unsure what to make of this, I dearly wish I knew,
Be gentle when you speak to me, I will do the same,
Hold me as you would a vase, of crystal as I came.

Life Cycle Of A Lobster Buoy

Born in the nursery of a salt water marsh,
An ecosystem brackish and harsh,
He feeds on the nutrients deep hidden there,
Beginning his life without a sea care,
In time he develops a hard wooden shell,
Often it's foam, though it's hard to tell,
When he is mature bright colors appear,
With striping marking his birth and the year,
Then one day when the flood is high,
He hugs his parents, nods goodbye,
Into the gulf of Maine he goes,
Precisely why, no one knows,
He hangs with the fishers, bobs on the sea,
Befriends all the lobsters, their bright designee,
When older he floats quite close to the shore,
Traverses the sand, a most difficult chore,
Then lives out his days on the side of a shack
With a band of buoys in a colorful stack,
Full facing the sun in a picturesque pod,
How they age is a wonder,
To some very odd.

Away Off Shore

My neighbor flew to Timbuktu,
My sibling sailed to Spain,
My cousin probed the Andes peaks
In blinding snow and rain,
My roommate flew to Fiji,
My uncle loved Bhutan,
A colleague from my place of work
Now travels all he can,
My sister dug for artifacts
In Brunei and Tangier,
Now she's off to Senegal,
Too close to home I fear,

I get their need for movement,
But why so close to home?
Why not travel farther still,
To Nantucket roam?
One may move one's body
Around in space and time,
Discover other cultures,
Enjoy another clime,
Yet those who travel farthest,
Those who travel more,
Pack up heart and mind and soul,
Then sail away off shore.

Cape Rain

Outside my bedroom window
The rhythmic rainfall sounds,
As fruitful, erotic, mirthful May
Makes her voluptuous rounds,

Her leaden sky, cozy and low,
Cousin to winter's drear,
I welcome her slate roof overhead,
Comforting not austere,

Our shingled cottage
Is silent,
Our hound now sound asleep,
Bunnies burrow beneath
Our deck,
I lie in my castle keep,

Lying abed with piles of books,
Thoughts beginning to slow,
Remember self, remember,
This is the best you will know,

My love has gone to Boston,
Our children are
Safely dispersed,
This is the apex of earthly joy
In which I am now immersed,

Lilacs bloom beside our deck,
New green grass grows apace,
Remember self, remember,
Do not this moment erase,

Life is an arc that rises and falls,
Returns all awakened
To slumber,
Self, mutable, transient self,
Fate still has your number,

Everything that you have today
Will in time soon fade,
Like our golden, summer sun
Will seek the winter shade,

At my upstairs window,
Relentless rainfall sounds,
Remember self, impermanent self,
Fate too is making her rounds.

Would You Rank A Minke Whale

Would you rank your children?
Would you parse out joy?
Would you take the things god made
And by comparison destroy
The exquisite uniqueness of each,
Be it womanhood or lovely beach?
Would you rank a Minke whale
Above a tall giraffe?
Would you praise a comely child
Then reduce by half
Your estimate of another?
Her sister or her brother?
Every woman that you meet,
Perfect as she came,
Like every strand along these shores
Each has an equal claim,
In god's eyes and in yours.

Beach Rules

No time, no clock,
No tick, no tock,
No news, no blues,
No crowd, no cloud,
No rip, no strip,
No burn, no churn,
No pine, no yearn,
No fraught, no ought,
No shark, no fin,
No when, no then,
No past, no future,
No problem, no matter,
No bane, no strain,
Not a chance of rain.

The Pirate Says

The cooler says, "reach in,"
The wave says, "I'm coming,"
The crab says, "here's a pinch,"
The jellyfish says, "here's a sting,"
The kite says, "higher,"
The mother says, "here's a snack,"
The lifeguard says, "be careful,"
The mermaid says, "you can't see me,"
The parking attendant says,
"This lot is full,"
The sandpiper says, "hurry, hurry,"
The dog says, "throw it,"
The breakwater says, "don't fall off,"
The shells say, "aren't we pretty,"
The one piece says, "I'm killin' it,"
The breeze says, "whoosh,"
The clouds say, "be patient,"
The moon says, "what am I doing here?"
The umbrella says, "flap, flap,"
The concoction says, "drink me,"
The sign says, "end of public beach,"
The pirate says, "I buried it
Around here somewhere."

Coastal Gifts To A Newborn

Kinship with the earth,
A vivid eye from birth,
Stout heart to thwart all pain,
Faith to deep content regain,
The opulence of joy,
Compassion to deploy,
Intrepid spirit, resiliency,
Impassioned curiosity,
Admired traits to exemplify,
Souls to love, be loved by,
A bit of wealth, a child, a spouse,
Equanimity of a seaside mouse,
A fervent quest and for the best,
A mind in service to the heart,
A blessed and unimpeded start.

Seaside Lullaby

Clarion shorebirds of the air
Temper your song, your cry, your care,
Alight on sand, slat fence, on bough,
My newborn sleeps beneath you now,
Buzzing insects of the yard
Stay your droning calling card,
Adopt a sleep-inducing hum,
Rough noise of day now overcome,
Songbirds of our coast and wood,
Chant softly in our neighborhood,
Sea breeze that blows from far away,
From off the Sound and Cape Cod Bay,
Your rousing rush of winds let fall,
Now sleeps, now sleeps,
My heart and all.

Double Baby Wave Jumping

Find two toddlers on the beach,
Take each child in hand,
Step carefully into the swirling surf,
Secure yourself in the sand,
Gauge the waves,
Their force, their height,
Time their flow, their crest,
Gentle waves with lesser might
Are usually the best,
Practice timing three together,
Synchronize each move,
If you wait and wait then jump,
You'll find the perfect groove,
Clever waves may try to trick
By slowing, peaking high
And never try to jump a wave
That quite obscures the sky,
If you get your leaps down pat
You'll soon forget the time,
Just thinking of the fun involved
I've quite forgot my rhyme.

Fast Ferry

She slips Hyannis harbor
In a slow and graceful arc,
With movements
Smooth and supple,
Her registered trademark,

You contemplate the shoreline
As it broadens then recedes,
Stake your claim
Along her stern,
Follow where she leads,

Then when she has
Cleared its mouth,
All little boats are past,
She rises on great haunches,
Shifts from slow to fast,

Two mighty jets roar to life,
Now agitate the sea,
Propelling all her passengers
To where they seek to be,
Nantucket Town,

Your view now is enchanting,
The panorama vast,
The Cape's low coast
Spreads far and wide,
Her stern rail you hold fast,

The sky itself enlarges,
Blue sea expands around,
The roar of her great engines
Creates a deafening sound,

Her wake now mesmerizes,
All foamy, white and churned,
You feel an inner vibrancy,
So pleased to have returned,

Sea birds dance behind her,
White sails slipstream her path,
Wild breezes play
With hair and clothes,
She has provoked their wrath,

In time you spy
The farther shore
As furious winds abate,
She makes a final dancer's turn,
You chat with your shipmate,

She glides into Nantucket Town,
A seaborne Fred Astaire,
Lowers you gently onto the wharf
Without an earthly care.

Shore Lines

Fathomless Sea

Some call you compassionless,
Cruel even,
Is that what you say I am?
Well are you?

I am not,
Neither am I benevolent,
I harbor no sympathy for you
Or the numberless creatures
That inhabit and surround me,
Neither have I ill intent,
I am merely the sea,
The fathomless sea,
Neither friend nor sworn enemy,
My birth ever hidden in mystery,

Though you seem intent to label me,
Before you seek to fathom mine,
Plumb your own depths as labyrinthine,
Some say your species is heartless,
Cruel even,
Are you?

Four Seasons

One for the body to run and play, dive and swim,
Make all of out of doors a gym,
A muscled season to move within,
Summertime, when all beach days are prime,

One for the heart, when reflective fall
Gives remembrance a start, when the past surfaces,
Longing floods the self and holidays rouse fellow feeling,
Autumn time, when the human heart is most sublime,

One for the mind, a colder season, the rational kind,
Clear, crisp, undistracted by feeling and play,
Season of nippy nights and daunting day,
Wintertime, when dreams retreat to a warmer clime,

One for the soul, as spring recovers what winter stole,
Giving the spirit wings,
Fruiting the land with burgeoning things and
Each waking soul with expectation,
Springtime, when hearts are gay, leaves are lime.

Jeweled Nights

My sister counted stars at night
While our parents dreamt,
My brother hoarded meteors
Which left his room unkempt,
I much preferred great galaxies,
Stacked each upon my bed,
While bouncing baby brother
Stuffed moonlight in his head,
A cousin carefully set the moon
Right atop the sea,
No matter where he found it
That's where it had to be,
A maiden aunt who stayed and played
Tried on Saturn's rings,
Wished for beaus, long love affairs,
Other wondrous things,
My sister's friend I must commend,
She often came to stay,
She rose upon the cool Cape air
To stroll the Milky Way,
We plucked from jeweled
Cape Cod nights
The most magical things we found,
Never did our parents stir,
Like us they were spellbound.

Wounded Sea

The rollicking, rolling, rapturous sea
Introduced herself to me,
Asked in a voice suffused with pain,
What did I ever hope to gain
By reducing her essence to words and verse?
Even paintings were to her a curse,
I asked her then what fault she found
From my tossing words around,
I only sought to capture soul,
But careless words had taken a toll,

How would I feel if she, one day,
Turned on me and tried to convey
All that I was or thought I was,
Or could be or would be or might be?
I pleaded my case on the open sand,
When the sea in reply made one demand,
And on that bracing, blue sky day
I heard the wounded sea to say:
Throw all your tainted tropes away,
Come bathe in me, my friend, this day.

Be Like Water

The mighty ocean,
Goddess of life,
Insinuates herself,
Envelops, surrounds,
Inundates,
Largely unobtrusive,
She seeks her own level,
Minds her own business,
Seeks the path
Of least resistance,
Yields if opposed,
Seldom contends
Unless prodded by wind,
Is persistent as well
And eternally patient,
Content to wait and wait,
Secretly erosive
She knows this is her planet,
Provides a nursery for life,
Teaches without preaching,
Subtly, gently
Conveys wise counsel
To all who give attention.

There Was A Time

A rogue onshore breeze
Startles me awake,
Shifts my agitated umbrella,
Rolls my beach towel
Into a tight ball
As thoughts of my elderly mother
Pop suddenly into my head,
Are thoughts of me
Now popping into hers?
Does such popping
Happen at the same time?

My children are grown,
Mother lives alone,
There was a time
She knew where I was
Every second,
Never out of her sight,
Out of her thoughts,
Out of her care,
Then I realize
She never took us to this beach,
How will she find me now?

This Coast Is Your Concern

Breathe you now her pure sea air?
This air is your concern,
Swim you 'neath her waters fair?
This water's your concern,
Feed you from her bounty here?
Her bounty's your concern,
Sail you now across her face?
This ocean's your concern,
Love you all her creatures here?
Their fate is your concern,
Tan you here beneath her sun
Till your swift span of life is done?
This coast is your concern.

Sunfish

Where is the rookery?
Where the breeding ground
Of these late spring newborns?
Within what estuary,
Within what hidden salt marsh
In the Cape's off season
Were they conceived?
By what magic do our own young know
That a new day-sail litter has arrived,
Adorned with fiberglass, pontoon hulls
And little, lateen sails?
I've seen them every summer in Wychmere
And Falmouth or running from Sesuit
To catch the wind off Cape Cod Bay,
Only to scurry back ahead of a menacing front,
Where is the hatchery?
Where the secret, wetland birthplace
Of these water babies,
These high summer breeze catchers?
And why do they cluster so
With their sunfish siblings?
No matter,
For now I'll let these mysteries be
And just enjoy my cygnets of the sea.

Picasso On The Sand

Picasso found himself on the sand,
Anxious, contorted, arms and legs akimbo
In a painfully compressed limbo,
Closer to taxed than relaxed and
Not quite sure how he got there,
Yet as the beach does its magic
He begins to slowly unwind,
His prominent privates retreat
To their wonted place lower down,
His head, rigid in an upright posture,
Long protruding from his right thigh,
Swings now high and
Happily reacquaints with his thick neck,
His two legs, sprouting from one shoulder
Find again their subordinate position
To the amazement of this beholder,
His amorous nose, long in
Carnal communion with eyes and mouth,
Repositions farther south,
While his bulging eyes migrate north
From feet and oddly misplaced thighs
Right before we bathers eyes,
Yet soon, like us, his days run out
Before he can fully untangle,
So he wisely plays a new angle
With those at work above his station,
And plaintively pleads for a longer vacation.

Great Pond Beach

Grant me the eternal peace of this place,
Its calmness and its generous grace,
It sonorous self-confidence, natural centeredness
And unperturbed beingness,

Grant me the integrity of this place,
The natural, cyclic harmony evident here,
The wordless reticence of this place
And leave in my soul not a single trace
Of the apprehension haunting our race,

Grant me too an acknowledgment
Of the divine favor here, the holy hush,
The incessant, universal thrum
That speaks to me, to everyone,
And says: to what is sacred
You will never be so near.

Harding's Beach

She appears and I scrutinize her sands,
Think her to death, as my classifying mind
Sorts her, chops her up, lays her reductively
Against a matrix of best, most and worst,
Scans and labels with a phalanx of adjectives,
Deconstructs her grain by grain, shell by shell,

Then, to subdue her further, five senses pounce,
Focusing obsessively on her sights, sounds,
Smells, taste and touch,
Should a single visit cause so much?
I analyze her salty mouth feel,
Note how her shorebirds,
Soar, glide, shriek and wheel,
How this day she strikes the ear and nose,
Whatever else my thinking mind can decompose,

Then and only then, after the mind in vain
Fails to make any true sense of her,
Do I find the off button and rout the mind,
Only then do I take her in
And find the peace I sought,
Without a single pressing thought,
Save the soul-engulfing, thrilling potency
Of her luminous, littoral beauty.

I Submit To You This Cape

Was it an unkind god
Gave us fretful brains?
A detached and toying god
Who let go all the reins?
Stranded us here
To fend for ourselves?
Was it a peevish god
Who set us in the dark of space?
A less powerful god?
Perhaps a god in lower case?
Or did we fall full out of grace
Forgetting when and how,
Perplexed within this mysterious now?

I think not, and since we have minds
Capable of choosing what to think,
What to feel, what is fiction, what is real,
I choose to embrace this probative evidence
Of cosmic benevolence, circumstantial,
Probative nonetheless:
Nature, love, family and as for nature
I submit to you this Cape
And her fantasy islands,
Which by curious happenstance
And uncanny, cosmic coincidence
Happened to be waiting here

In this time, this place,
For me and thee to find,
Ignore the mind,
The Greeks were wrong,
Better to be born.

Imagine You're A Sea Star

Imagine you're a sea star, supine, in full view,
Five limbs splayed out in symbolic communion
With your heavenly cousins, waiting to be admired,

Imagine you're a whale, sole sovereign of the sea,
Massive, moving effortlessly, unimpeded by gravity,
Grave thoughts even, gliding, breaching,
Blowing your top, letting off steam,
Fully immersed in your liquid element,

Imagine you're a blue crab, clattering sideways,
Raising great claws to pinch invasive toes
That randomly plunge down at you
Through the sun-glistening water,

Imagine you're a jellyfish, squishy, floating,
Half submerged, translucent, with delicate tendrils
Trailing behind and down, waiting with a little shock
For those inclined to view your diaphanous,
Translucent beauty as weakness,

Imagine you're a barnacle snug against a sea-facing boulder,
Part of a cluster daily washed vigorously
By predictably attentive tides,
Then lovingly dried in the sun, with little interest
In being uniquely different from your mates,

Imagine you're a sea creature imagining its own Creator
Without flaw or blemish of any kind,
Seeing itself as a splendid, impeccable version of each,
Blown into this watery world in your own god's image,
Watched over till you leave it,

Then imagine how many awe-inspiring,
Pelagic gods there must be,
Or how many miraculous facets
To the One.

Something In The Water

Come into the water timid child,
Nothing here is wicked, wild,
See how the sun peers right through
To open up a clearer view,

Step carefully here, banish fear,
Come watch your mother swim,
Yet nothing that his mother said
Could his suspicions dim,

There's something there, I know there is,
Hidden 'neath the sand,
Hungry things that snatch and grab,
Tug at foot and hand,

You cannot live your life that way,
You mustn't live in fear,
She smiled, reached out to take his hand,
Wipe away a tear,

He took a step, soon was in,
She dove then swam ahead,
While every step the young boy took
Engorged his heart with dread,

It's got me mom, I knew it would,
He cried, then disappeared,
Quick taken by the hideous thing
Her timorous boy had feared.

Too Much Here To Amuse

Whine with me I wailed to the waves,
Not a chance they said,
What more could crashing rollers crave?
As on and on they sped,

Fuss with me I fumed to the fish,
Not a chance they said,
We swim all day then go to school,
Quite soon will be well read,

Bemoan with me I begged the breeze,
Not a chance it said,
We blow, we wander as we please,
This coastline overspread,

Sigh with me I said to the sun,
Not a chance it said,
I track across this gorgeous sky
Then climb fatigued to bed,

Will no one match my misery?
I need to sing the blues,
Not a chance the beach replied,
Too much here to amuse.

The Children Of Chatham

They're stalking the children of Chatham,
Pulling them into the bay,
Feasting upon their plump, little limbs,
Spurting up roseate spray,
Bored with familiar, seaborne snacks,
Weary of fatty, old seals,
The great whites circle her shoreline
Craving dainty, diminutive meals,
They wait for distracted, new mommies
To absent themselves for a bit,
Then tear at the fleshy, ripe morsels
Who fall into the sea from the spit,
At first the wide-eyed, young lovelies
Gurgle and smile at the whites,
Thinking their row of bicuspids
Is one of the summer's delights,
Then, in a foamy red flash they're gone,
Ripped apart head and limb
As other tasty, plump Chathamites
Tumble into the sea for a swim,
Yet for all of the salty commotion,
The town is not yet at a loss
For more than enough bouncy babies remain
Despite all the infantile cost,
Locals have been heard to say
Why Chatham and not Wellfleet?
Are not their babes as savory and fresh,

An equally tasty treat?
In time warm summer's eclipsed by fall,
New babes are held as reserves,
While the sated sharks dream long in the sea
Of next year's delightful hors d'oeuvres.

Imposters

Imposters ape our splendid Cape,
Synthetic shores bent out of shape,
Cobbling together with masking tape,
Diminutive dunes, a rough moonscape,
Into a bric-a-brac seascape,
While ours yet merits ticker tape,
With peerless sands, exquisite shape,
While theirs advises quick escape,
Quiet laughter, a witty jape,
Most everyone who strolls unshod
Would give the true, objective nod
To fair and salty old Cape Cod,
Fashioned by an act of god.

Introvert

Like an ascetic she moves quietly away,
Farther down the sulfurous beach,
Beneath the molten sun, well beyond the reach
Of their games and aimless chatter,
Their assertive, noisy densities,
Happily burdened as she is
With introverted propensities,
Yet not so asocial as to avoid the beach
Or miss its sensual self-indulgence or
The sunny exhilaration of a high-summer day,
Or miss, as well, a chance to once again define
Herself as one apart, perhaps without the requisite
Heart or democratic tolerance to connect,
And she sometimes suspects
They too proudly define themselves
In assertive, gregarious, deafening opposition
To her reflective, solitary tribe as well,
Nature too, she privately observes,
Recoils at their invasive music and loud talk,
As silently disapproving gulls back away,
High strung terns, in unison,
Retreat hurriedly in little quicksteps,
And unshaven seals, peeking from just offshore,
Shake their baby-faced heads at the cacophony,
While a single, regal, judgmental cormorant,
Drying her black wings, silently rebukes them,
As do her own censorious, unvoiced thoughts,
Before she settles in, alone and comfortably apart,
To reconnect with her inner being,

And commiserate with the too tolerant, offended,
Matchless beach, invisible to these others,
Though here now arrayed in all its
Ineluctable finery.

Just Above The Lovely Sea

How kind of evolution
To place the sky right where it is,
Just above the lovely sea
Whose placement pleases equally,
How considerate of her
To carve this darling dune,
Without a single, clear intent
From all consciousness immune,
How caring of her
To fashion creatures,
So varied, so complex,
How odd that certain questions
Our human minds still vex,
How thoughtful of such
A heartless thing
To bring to nearly everything
A meaningless aesthetic,
Without the need to conjure up
A Maker, how pathetic,
How clever of a kind of science
To demonstrate such self reliance,
I do admire evolution's skill
And unique, unassisted ability
To mold a winsome world at will,
But why evolve a human mind
That senses some intent behind?

A Cleansing Breath

While swimming on the first day
I caught a cleansing breath,
I had eluded all of those
Who'd made a kind of death
Of my work life,
The egotists, the sticklers,
The two faced and the proud,
The sycophants, the slackers,
The vengeful and the loud,
Yet as I looked around me,
Soon realized that I
Had not evaded anyone,
They swam as well nearby,
Then came to me a second thought
More bracing than the first,
What if those who shrink from us
Now feel themselves accursed
To find us splashing next to them
In this same sea immersed?

La Plage Il Ne Déçoit Jamais

Romance may disappoint,
The fates may not anoint,
Shared blood may disenchant,
Lovers may recant,
Ones allies may thee thwart,
Betrayal as a sport,
Bosses may frustrate,
Fortune comes too late,
The self may thee delude,
Your tribe may thee exclude,
Waiters may be rude,
Clouds may the sun occlude,
Strangers may mislead,
Friends you may misread,
Colleagues may deceive,
Now time for a reprieve,
For as the French say:
The beach,
She never disappoints.

Laughing Buddha

He was four or so
And his enormous, canary yellow trunks
Went all the way from his belly
To his ankle,
He didn't care, ill-fitting clothes
Could never rankle,
For he was the sea's,
And the sand's,
And the sun's,

His doting mother beamed
On him from her sandy perch
Five feet away and
Not a word did I hear him say
All that perfect day,

He radiated pure happiness,
Standing in his small, new body
On the edge of the sea,
As though he was simply
Glad to be,
Unlike the rest of us
Who make such a fuss
Of relaxing on the sand,

She handed him a large
Blue pail,
Which he grabbed
With pudgy fingers,

He waded in,
Filled it to the brim,
Then promptly emptied it
In one full, joyous flush
Over his own head,
Then wore the pail
Tight and low over his eyes
Like a drum major,
With its plastic handle
Flapping against his chest,

He blindly marched a few steps
After each baptism
In and out of the surf,
His mother admired
His filling the pail,
Yet was always looking away
When he emptied it
Over his head,

Perhaps she'd witnessed
This sacrament before,
I concluded he did all this repeatedly
In order to bless the beach,
Never was it so properly blessed
Or a new, little man
So properly baptized
Over and over again,
For he was the sea's,
And the sand's,
And the sun's.

Another Way To Be

Something tense inside of me,
Holding on too tight you see,
Something forced with human will,
Rigid, less adaptable,
Something fixed without flex,
Something that my soul doth vex,
When the sun, sand, air and sea
Modeled another way to be,

The sun when blocked turns aside,
Shifting sand's the norm,
The air if stymied continues to glide,
While the sea just assumes a new form,

Upon such thoughts I soon let go
With a loud shout of "eureka!"
Such things will often happen here
To cheer the earnest seeker,

Now like the sun, I welcome shade,
Like the sand, I shift,
Like the air, for pliancy was made,
Now like the sea, I drift.

The Boy Who Sailed To Monomoy

There was a boy from Harwich
Who sailed to Monomoy,
He loved his mother, loved his dad,
Whose hearts he filled with joy,
But he was plagued with wanderlust,
His head all stuffed with dreams,
So one fine day he rigged his boat,
Caulked along its seams,
He rose before the sun did,
Slipped slowly into the Sound,
Set a course for Monomoy,
Carefully looked around,
Until he spied a pod of seals
Who waved at him with glee,
He waved right back,
Moored his boat and
Lived there near the sea,

The seals were quite elated,
They tossed him in the air,
They swam, they sang,
They nuzzled him
And warned him to beware
Of the sharks,
One day a seal with pangs of guilt
Suggested he return,
His parents surely missed their boy,
Were filled with much concern,
But he could never leave his friends,

Nor would their friendship spurn,
His parents finally found their boy,
Sailed over every day,
Since they were loath to end his joy,
He lives there still today.

Loaves & Fishes

Dragged by the youngest
Up and over the dune,
Down along the molten sand
One clement day in June,
Came the capacious cooler,
Red and white, loaded down
With treats of every kind,
It held enough to feed the beach,
With great morsels left behind
For the scavengers,
The boy collapsed upon the sand,
Struggled to catch his breath,
While all bathers munched away
He came quite close to death,
All that day his bountiful box
Disgorged its hidden treasure,
Earth's deepest, widest cache of food
By any normal measure,
It fed their group, fed the beach,
And as the sun set low,
Still greedy hands within did reach
Yet soon was time to go,
The weary boy revived himself,
Grabbed his treasure chest,
Lugged and pushed it over the sand,
Leaving me to digest
The kind of sorcery I had seen
One temperate day in June,
When a single cooler fed the beach
One miraculous afternoon.

Why Preserve This Fabled Shore

Why preserve this fabled shore
That will in time erode?
Why conserve when to consume
Will no one discommode?
Why maintain its pristine state
That hasn't been that way of late?
Seems itself to regulate?
What kind of penalty might ensue
To me, to mine, to you,
If you and I enjoy this view
Then leave it in distress?
What to us can future do
If we bequeath a mess?
Yet still a voice within my head
Pipes up with this to say:
If we despoil our heaven here
There may be hell to pay.

Look To The Clam

Look to the clam to hold your tongue,
To the lobster for good taste,
Look to the crab to defend yourself,
Sea snails to remedy haste,
Look to the heron for grace and poise,
To the schools to synchronize,
Take counsel from all the creatures here
If you seek to be prudent and wise,
Look to the bottlenose for play,
To the whale to let off steam,
Look to the shark to learn to survive,
To the gull for self esteem,
Look to the barnacle to bond,
To dream, the tan sea star,
Each creature has a message for you,
Each an exemplar.

An Instant Deep Rapport

My child came with me to the beach,
I marveled at her skill,
As she communed with fauna there
From whales to tiny krill,
She had a way with animals,
An instant, deep rapport,
They read her heart, she read theirs,
In seacoast semaphore,
I watched her lift a fiddler crab,
Chat away with ease,
She shouted then a bright hello
To puffins on her knees,
She gave high fives to humpbacks
Who blew their spouts in turn,
No creature hiding in the deep
Would she ever spurn,
She shared her thoughts with herons,
Seagulls, ospreys, terns,
Reaped for herself, all creatures too,
What amiability earns,
She greeted five limbed starfish,
Conversed with sharks and cod,
Impressed us all, Triton as well,
The critter's trident god,
She motioned to engage a ray,
I told her not today,
But dad, she said with deep insight,
He has so much to say.

Economies Of Scale

Opinions are rife
Concerning beach life,
With the mind
Hot to venture
Its thoughts,
If you would avoid
All cognitive strife
Pay heed to this king
Of bon mots:
Calories in,
Calories out.

The Age Of Sail

Why do I see them, hear them,
All along the Great Beach
Amidst the thickening fog,
Stepping happily out of the surf,
Blasted by spindrift, rough waves,
Relieved, laughing,
Chattering amongst themselves,
Clad in ancient apparel,
Pleased to be on dry land,
Embracing one other,
Disgorged by the sea
And a cloaking mist
Which nightly sets them free?

Why do I see them, hear them
Brushing past me on their way
To the footpaths that rise
Through the lofty escarpment?
Hapless, diaphanous victims of the age of sail,
Each a tragic tale,
Children, mothers, fathers, workers, sailors,
Thrown into the deep with Neptune's jailors
As their clippers split and foundered,
Severing each from families, lovers and life,
So close to shore, to the hearth, to refuge,
Forgotten, deep-fathomed souls long confined,

Mercilessly left behind,
Till the pitying fog nightly comes
To set them free,
For ears like mine to hear,
For eyes like mine to see.

Coastal Kingdoms

Oh the variety here, the amazing, astonishing,
Miraculous variety, wherever you look,
Wherever you step, come put your head into the water,
Cast your eyes upon the air,
Crouch low and gaze upon the flats and rocks,
Witness the remarkable salmagundi here,
Seemingly limitless, boundless in size, in appearance, in design,
All the fishes, all the plants,
All the shorebirds, red and green seaweeds,
The untamable, propagating wildflowers,
Trees, shrubs and grubs, amphibians, arthropods,
Reptiles, all co-existing for a time, engaged
As predator and prey, night and day,

What an Imagination gifted our world with such
Variety, you must at least grant that,
You who look for culprits, clues and causation,
Each creature distinguished from the other
Through movement, burrowing, flying, leaping,
Crawling, creeping, clothed in skins, scales, feathers and fur,
Each with brains and hearts, circulatory parts,
Each with distinctive dwelling places,
Each armed with unique means of attack and defense,
Omnivores and scavengers with singular sounds
And mating rituals,

Oh yes, here the tree of life is rife, and
Today I will immerse myself in its astonishing variety,
Delight myself with the gift it is, and
Although I may not come to any conclusions,
I will cherish all that my senses here perceive,
Work sedulously and with gratitude to Whomever
To preserve it for the unborn future,

Lest through negligence and inattentiveness
There be an indelible mark against me,
Entered by a meticulous, celestial Scrivener
In some secret, permanent, perpetual ledger.

Make From All Of These The Shore

Take this dancing beach grass, these blue-black barnacles,
Seabird nesting areas and bullhead lilies,
These foredunes, anxious alewives and fiddler crabs,
Great green marshes, migrating sea ducks,
Myriad mudflats and parabolic dunes, these
Mislaid mermaid's purses, sweet muscled scallops,
Warm, eddying currents, swooping scoters,
Wetlands, stationary fronts and more,
And make from all of these the shore,
As I did, give it a go, you know, the old empyrean try,
See if what you make of them pleases soul and eye,
I'll bet you make a hash of it,

Here, take these mollusks, these spiny sea urchins,
These pretty periwinkles, then mix in the sandy
Substrate and all the coastal habitats,
Gales and sails, seaweeds and algae too,
See if what you make of them is worth the view,
I'll bet you make a hash of it, leave everything askew,
If it's any consolation, evolution would have too.

Before The Next High Tide

Should you rent or own?
Consign your heart to him or her?
Seek new employment or recommit?
Come clean or keep your counsel?
Confront or yield? attend or decline?
Whatever your question the water's fine
For finding an answer,

Come on in or walk along,
No little questions please,
Like what's for lunch,
Or cosmic queries like
How many gods there are or
Who gives light to every star?

Keep to the middle,
The practical questions,
Those that directly concern you,
Those are best for the beach,

Pose your single question early,
Silently, with an open heart
And a child's full faith,
Let the beach ponder it,
Give it time while you play,
While you idle all the day,

In time you'll have your answer,
The beach will soon confide
In you her doting dancer
Before the next high tide.

Moshup

Rules that apply on a textile beach
Are generally few, well within reach,
You may look where you want, wear what you will,
Tucked up good and tight or in chic dishabille,
Gendarmes won't harm you or move you along,
Unmolested, unbothered, all summer long,
But the rules that apply on a birthday suit beach
Are many and random, often far out of reach,
Do you pay like the others, park in a lot,
Though a suit and a towel you might have forgot?
Do you hide in the dunes, high up on a bluff,
Concealing your assets while you tan in the buff?
Do you look where you want, will binoculars serve,
Or will such behavior the neighbors unnerve?
Is flashing for lightning, full mooning for night?
If you knew all the rules would you still get it right?
When you're fully divested, unadorned in the raw,
Can others be sure what they claim that they saw?
This verse could go on, now it's time to sum up,
When you're on a free beach, just remember,
Eyes up.

Mermaids Of Howes

They dance in the early morning
At the farthest end of the beach
In a spectral fog of sea-green mist
Beyond all human reach,
They slip away when the waking sun
Reveals their sheltered bay,
After an hour of watery fun,
That's what the locals say,
They skip from the water onto the beach,
Onto the bars to play,
Sway in a circle holding hands
Until the break of day,
Each one young and beautiful,
Each with lustrous hair,
Most of them sopranos,
A contralto here and there,
They sense when a human is present,
Slip slowly back into the deep,
If ever you happen to see one
You must her secret keep,
If you doubt the truth of my story
Take a stroll along Howe's sand,
Be alert and auditory,
Walk straight to the end of the land,
There atop the large sea stones
Uncovered by the tide,
Beneath their eddying, emerald manes

Howe's merry mermaids hide,
Step lightly, don't disturb their sleep
Or touch their billowing hair,
They need to believe they can't be seen
Asleep in their sandy lair.

Message In A Bottle

Two young beachcombers
Discovered a sodden, faded parchment
Many years ago on this very beach,
Unable to decipher it,
Or make any sense at all out of it, they
Sealed it once again within its old bottle,
Tossed it back into the waves,
And for some minutes watched it float away,

As told to me, here is what was written thereon:

"The powers not delegated to the United States
By the Constitution, nor prohibited by it to the States,
Are reserved to the States respectively,
Or to the people."

On the parchment to the right in cryptic marginalia
Was added this mysterious, nearly indecipherable line
In an old man's shaky, cursive script:

"If you can keep it,
Benjamin."

Please Sir I Want Some More

The very moment that my breathing slows,
That my heart stops racing,
That my fevered mind moderates its incessant chatter,
That my obsessiveness begins to wane,
That my knotted muscles relax
And happily assume their natural shape,
That my flotilla of fears begins to disperse,
That my sense of responsibility finds
Delightful, insubordinate charm in unaccustomed
Dereliction of duty,
That my futile ordering of life
Surrenders to chance, surprise,
And a wise acceptance of impermanence,
It is at that precise moment
That my vacation comes to an abrupt end,
A shockingly, jarringly sudden quietus,
And the cavalier cruelty of a trickster universe
Becomes alarmingly apparent to me
Once again.

Muse Of The Dunes

Predawn stillness and
The dormant dune shack
Begins to breathe,
While within this castaway
Creative demons seethe,
My lounging hound, aging jowls
Resting on two ivory paws,
Lazily waves his white-tipped tail,
As all-embracing, morning quiet
Defers the fevered, human wail,
Is it time?

A slender, alluring, mischievous muse
By name of Erato,
Thin-hipped, bare, vaporous, diffuse,
Descends step by stealthy step
Down along the steepy face of the dune,
Sprawls atop my lap,
Brashly looks me in the eye,
Drapes her locks across a thigh,
Whispers in soft tones sublime,
"Seacoast seer earn your time,
Channel through me, dreamer,"
Till my pen begins to write
With second sight to earn my life
And reclaim yours.

My Barefoot Rounds

I come to the beach to clear my head,
When work and care have left for dead
The joy and ease I used to know
When I possessed a youthful glow,
When I just lived, did not plan,
Before the advent of the man,

I come to the beach in the early morn
When the promising day is still new born,
When first she tries her scents and sounds,
It's then I make my barefoot rounds,
Press footprints in her slushy sands,
On my mind make no demands,

Her welcome is for me alone,
No chat, companion, telephone,
I return again at her golden time
When the angled sun is past its prime,
Cloaking her dunes in an amber cast,
When commotion of day is blessedly past,

Everything comes within ones reach
At the proper time on a favorite beach,
Everything becomes quite clear
When the surf and the sea and the sand are near,
When the mind's tight hold begins to release
And the bountiful beach imparts its peace.

Musings At Surfside Beach

Nothing can touch you here on earth
Once you tame the mind,
Font of suffering from your birth,
Scourge of all mankind,

Nothing can harm you here below
Once you find the key,
That turns the lock from pain to joy,
Sets every human free,

Nothing should distress you
From first clean breath to last,
Creation's here to bless you,
Wellsprings of joy are vast,

Mind's master now resolve to be,
Not victimized by thought,
Control the ebb and flow and see
What untamed thoughts have wrought,

Release your spirit, it harbors joy,
Waits on your resolve
To mind-created pain destroy,
All angst and fear dissolve,

Nothing can touch you here below
Once you find the key,
Decide today to free yourself
From mind and misery.

Where Is The Home Of The Salt-Spray Rose

Where is the land of the hardy beach plum?
Where does the beach heather grow?
Where is the home of the salt-spray rose?
They told me you might know,

Where are the starfish that fell from the sky?
Where are the heart-shaped stones?
Where are the views that pleasure the eye?
Old shipwrecks shaped like bones?

I could tell you the place where the beach pea
Blooms, where the dunes loom over the sea,
But there's an excess of peace and quiet there,
A surfeit of serenity,

Let me think of a place you might prefer
More than our calm ocean shelf,
Where the action is fast and furious
And you'll never run into yourself.

Rising With Aplomb From A Beach Chair

Rising with aplomb is hardly the norm,
So plan it carefully and dispel the notion
That rising in one fluid motion
Will suffice, so my advice
Is to toss a book onto the sand
Just out of reach to your right,
And while pretending to grab it,
Tip your chair slowly onto the sand
With you in it, then wait a minute
For some standard beach commotion,
Like a swimmer in extremis
Or a great white in the ocean, and
As bathers eyes from you do stray,
Discretely push your chair away
To its original upright position,
Then lie prone till end of day,
When few will see you try to stand
And graceless on your bottom land.

Ode To A Salt Marsh

O false, seaside meadow full of seeming serenity,
O featureless form, shunning with subtle, briny aplomb
The distant drama of the shoreline, where prideful dunes,
Bombastic waves and a braggart sun compete
For the active vacationer's attention,
Their bumptious bluster more the coastal norm,
O half hidden, hostile, horizontal habitat,
Flushed twice daily by the rush of sea salt
In forceful flood and slow retreat,
I, for one, see beneath the trickery of appearances,
Your nature's clever duplicities,
How you hide your innumerable creatures
Competing as prey and predator, hunter and hunted,
Do not imagine that your brief remove
From the coast itself or the conspiratorial complicity
Of estuaries and barrier beaches
Gives you sufficient concealment,
Yet fear not, I will not out you to our unconscious,
Inattentive world so keen on urgent rest and
Refreshing respite, and instead shall maintain
Your hard won deceptions,
Keep your secrets safe from true perceptions,
And in delicious solitude I shall permit my
Tranquility seeking spirit to soar across your broad,
Green swath of gently swaying cord grass,
Let my oppressed, urban ears become finely attuned
To your subtle, nocturnal music, your avian melodies,
Your buggy buzz and hum,
Let my rough, myopic vision broaden and acclimate

To the wondrous variety of your species, your shorebirds,
Minute mollusks, neonate fishes and willful, wanton wildflowers,
And too, your gregarious greenheads,
And one day at the first sight of a red winged,
My soul may well take flight and alight somewhere
Within you, and I will beg you then to teach me
Your eternal secrets of unflappability and concealment,
So I too may present a convincingly false, unruffled face
To the soul-assaulting world I wander in.

No Place Special

Once on the Cape & Islands, my strangulated heart
Like a high flying, multicolored, freedom loving kite,
Dances and plays wantonly in the high breeze
Over a line of sand-corniced dunes,
My dulled senses eagerly awake
To a feast of seaside, sensual stimulation,
My shallow breath eases, swells with the sweet sea
Air, my anxious, hard won sleeps deepen,
And my unsettling, Miro-like dreamtime
Is replaced by paradisiacal imaginings,
My pinched soul, now limitless as the heavens,
Finds joy and with the immensity of the sea and sky,
Sufficient space to soar and gleefully expand,
My deadened imagination sprouts broad wings,
Happily glides over the marching whitecaps
With the arresting grace of a majestic shorebird,
My too sullen spirit finds deep peace
And instant affinity with all of nature,
My intimacies regain a long lost vibrancy and
Set binary starlight to sparkle in my lover's eyes,
And as my urban misanthropy wanes,
All human flaws are transmuted, as in a fairy tale,
Into nothing more than charming foibles,
Petty peccadillos not unlike my own,
Inviting compassion and deserved forgiveness,
Yet back at work, when asked where I had gone,
I replied: "no place special, just to the shore."

My Vineyard

I remember you well
From glorious summers past,
Shoulder seasons while they did last,
My isolated, island realm,
Unrivaled, beloved of nature,
Your variety of views, special hues,
Seven miles offshore yet still more
The lands than the seas,
With enough of an ocean trip to please,
Your southern shoreline
Bracing itself against the Sound
To inhibit further seaward drift,
A country to yourself I found,
Up island to Chilmark or down to Edgartown,
How soon a visitor forgets your island
Soul, when ambling round your woods and
Fields, yet how quickly that same visitor is
Reminded, when every inner inland ramble
Leads back to the encircling sea
And its palpable sense of eternity,
Open to all, democratic, welcoming,
Preserving nature's bounty, god's art
And man's comforts in an enviable equilibrium,
Midsummer memory maker extraordinaire,
Whose maritime sights and sounds,
Sprinkling of quaint villages
And pluperfect harbors
Carve deep furrows in the mind,

Yet leave a poignant sense of loss behind
For all who must depart,
Oh yes, I remember you well,
My heavy heart's restorative,
My vision of an island
My Vineyard.

My Nantucket

I remember you well,
More the seas than the lands,
When seen from above speeding south,
Trying vainly to gain distance from the mainland,
Putting out farther to sea in your own salty,
Seafaring mind, spare, grey, fog-enshrouded,
Hunkered down in gales and wintry blows,
Your elegant town center harkening back
To an earlier time, your choice, white beaches
Each as wonderfully different and diverting
As the women I loved and still do,
Your prismatic rainbows saluting passing storms,
Sea-sculpted geometry of Coatue,
Your chattering migratory flocks,
Handsome red-transomed trawlers,
Weathered decks, dune slat fencing,
Your cozy, bunkered solitariness,
Elegant, proper, cozy, cobblestoned core,
Your stoic self-possession, standoffishness,
Lonely, steadfast bravery
And red brick Georgian pride,
I see you now in your sou'wester,
Leaning into the driving rain and wind,
Mimicking Mother Nature in your patience,
Your stoicism, your doggedness,
Oh yes, I remember you well,
My coastal consolation, seaside solace,
My dream of an island,
My Nantucket.

Whose House Is That Upon The Rise

Whose house is that upon the rise, proud stands above the bay?
Whose mansion there upon the neck, so private, far away?
Whose cottage fit for royalty, moored like an ocean liner?
I never spied a better home along the coast that's finer?

And those upon the islands, most with private beach,
Massive, envied, well-appointed, all beyond my reach,
Each with turrets, porticos, pools and splendid views,
From year to year I asked myself, which one might I choose?

Whose boat is that upon the bay with lines so sleek and fine?
Whose sailing ship with handsome looks? I wish that she were mine,
Whose yacht with lovely keel and prow, snug cabins just for rest?
I think of all the boats I've seen, perhaps she is the best,

I now own neither house nor boat, nor have I means to gain,
My coveting was a curious thing that only caused me pain,
Do owners sleep a deeper sleep, enjoy a better view?
Are they more intimate with the sea than I as bather knew?
Are they warmer 'neath the sun, with such things more blissed?
One day it dawned upon my soul, no blessings had I missed,

Today I mouth a silent prayer, all desiring laid to rest,
Go my way with merry heart, contented, self-possessed.

Vineyard Versifier

Free verse fell out his pockets,
Scattered on the ground,
Was by eager readers read
Wherever it was found,
His verse was like a torrent
Overflowing banks,
Undeterred by berms and dikes,
So broad it had no flanks,
Free verse fell out his teeming brain,
Filled up the empty page,
Absent rhyme, meter, form,
Yet everywhere the rage,
His verse was fecund, fertile,
True as random thought,
Pure and unrestricted
As ever bard begot,
Yet now he has this growing fear
That what he thought was free
Is dear,
That what he may have lost
Is its true cost to the reader.

The National Seashore

Come see The Works,
Put aside your hymnals,
Your catechism and
Heal the schism
Between nature and your god,
How odd that
You that don't see his face,
Her countenance,
In such a favored place,
Her symmetry, His beauty,
Your oft-neglected duty,

Come see The Works,
Leave your sterile house of prayer,
Not all that's holy there,
Come see what puts stained glass
To shame,
No humble human soul can name,

Come see The Works,
All sanctified,
Seems they lied who deified,
Put all your gods indoors,
Confined by buttress, spires, vaults,
Bare, cold and stony floors,
Come see The Works,
All yours.

Nauset Night

She pulled my jacket round her,
Wild winds began to blow,
She took my hand in hers
And smiled,
And with our heads bent low,
Stepped into the murky mist
Of Nauset Beach
As far as we could go,

Salt spray from off the ocean,
Cool sand beneath bare feet,
The rhythmic roar of distant surf
Did with our thoughts compete,

What magic here,
What mystery too,
What threat beyond our ken,
As Nauset Light swept
O'er the sea
Time and time again,

A spectral light,
A warning light for men,
That Nauset now was
Not for us,
As in bright day had been,

We trudged along the crown
Of beach,
Embracing as we went,
Walking into danger now,
We knew its special scent,

She glanced at me,
I looked at her,
We'd gone quite far enough,
The only humans on this strand
Of foggy, arcane stuff,

Yet mixed with wariness
And fear,
With such raw ocean power near,
We felt communion with the night,
Black sea, white stars,
And ghostly light,

For within us both did course
That very same uncanny force
That lit the stars,
Lurked in the sea,
Enveloped all in mystery,

We left the beach hand in hand,
Mute, in silent awe,
No words could frame
Our wonder,
Or tell just what we saw.

Newcomb Hollow Beach

Rise, oh rise, you nearly dead,
Rise up from off your dying bed,
Flee your hospice, leave your home,
Come tonight to wild Newcomb,
Unfasten all your drips and leads,
For dying here far exceeds
A meek departure in your bed,
Fly, fly upon her sea instead,

Come now from out your nursing home
To gale-swept, wild and dark Newcomb,
Chose your death, your dying breath,
Don't let it feeble come,
Hurl yourself upon her waves,
Give a decent, final run,
Across her dunes, her chilly sand,
Then when storm and wind command,
With one last hurtle, high and free,
Commend your soul to god and sea.

Night Winds

Cape & Islands are asleep,
So too the Bay and mighty deep,
The Sound though fitful slumbers well
And only those awake can tell
That Aeolus has roused the winds,
The calmer daytime oft rescinds,
Boreas wafts from off the Bay,
Eurus from the Sea,
Notus from the silent Sound,
Zephyrus west of me,
Their fresh air floods the darkened sky,
Conspires with Morpheus by and by
To deepen every dreamer's sleep,
Comfort those now counting sheep,
Some winds run along the coast,
Others well inland,
All scent the Cape & Islands here
At Aeolus' command,
While heaping praise upon her days
Do not forget her nights,
When cool and ocean-scented air
Upon the coast alights.

Nobska Point Beach

A sullen sun loiters in the sky today,
Full of discontent, malaise, grumbling
As she contends with callous clouds that
Each invasive front now sends
To obscure her gilded beams,
See how they steal a march
On her royal rays,
Hamper her, discomfort her,
Eclipse her sky queen throne,
Sending battalions of bathers home,
Yet in her enterprising way
She brightens now and then today,
Seizing on the gaps and breaks
Every passing cloud line makes,
Plucky she is, ever resourceful,
Dispersing shadow and shade
Each encroaching confluence
Of clouds has made,
She routs their downdrafts,
Thwarts their screen,
Looks for ways to dive between,
Now mauling billows high unseen, then
With one last trick up her sleeve
She does the dappled day retrieve,
Now parts the proud and swollen clouds
To welcome back her tanning crowds.

Something Is Amiss

This beach appears the same today
Yet something is amiss,
The creatures all around it seems
Have misplaced all their bliss,
Bathers too have morphed as well,
All now suffused with joy,
Have banished fear, anxiety,
A new centeredness deploy,
It seems we've traded places
With creatures lower down,
Whose customary dignity
Has won them great renown,
They don't appear like us to fear,
To worry, whine or brood,
Or suffer from a discontent
In thrall to every mood,
They are themselves
Which we are not,
Secure within their skin,
While we with anxious, manic minds
Scarce let our lives begin,
Perhaps at last we've learned from them
A wiser way to be,
Enjoy our lives, live out our days
Without apology.

Ode To The Lobster Roll

Thou tender, scarlet, most succulent crustacean,
When declawed, when devoured,
Most deserving recipient of global approbation,
How modest, how humble you appear,
Yet how dear, how very dear,
Snug within your lightly grilled and buoyant bun
Beneath a thin, oleaginous veneer,
I venerate your mound of meat, tail and knuckle
Which causes even the strong to buckle,
How yearned for in the frozen season
Giving the shivering soul a reason
To dream of elusive summer,
How prepossessing, petulant, coy, flirtatious,
Yet when devoured how impressively gracious,
How you taunt me, toy, play games,
Knowing how your meaty, tender flesh inflames,
How disdainful of faux filler you are,
Specious salad, false base,
Of deceiving lettuce merely a trace,
Lunch for Kings, repast for Queens,
Not restricted to those of means,
Be there for me my tasty friend
Whene'er my appetite requires,
This missive of deep affection I send
To the one who stokes my fires,
Come now, come near,
My famished heart console,
Too sweet, dear sweet, lobster roll.

Prayer For Coastal Stewardship

Make me an instrument of Your preservation,
Where there is habitat degradation
Let me sow renewal,
Where there is acidification, purification,
Where there is erosion, reclamation,
Where there is defilement, cleansing,
Where there is desecration, consecration,
Where there is noise, stillness,
Where there is extinction, rejuvenation,
Where there is overfishing, replenishment,
Where there is unconscious pollution,
Conscious awareness,
Where there is ugliness, beautification,

Grant that I may not so much
Consume as to conserve,
Exhaust as to pass on,
Plunder as to maintain,
Squander as to perpetuate,
For it is through such preservation
That we honor all creation
And hold these seaside sanctuaries
In sacred trust for posterity.

On The Bass River Bridge

"Shall I write of beauty or truth?"
I asked a fisher one day,
While he was casting on the flood,
I think I heard him say:
"If you write of truth, young man,
You'll stand on shaky ground,
The moment that you stake a claim
It's opposite will sound,
Truth is all perspective,
Angle, point of view,
An often-futile exercise
That cleaves our world in two,
Yet if you write of beauty,
Far more consensus there,
Far less disputation,
Much less doctrinaire,"
He cast his rod a second time
Letting more line out,
What then the fisher said to me,
Rings true without a doubt,
"Write something beautiful today,"
Is what I heard the fisher say.

High Modernist Bemoans The Cape & Islands

Battered berms of shattered shells,
Whose dispersed, decrepit domiciles were these?
I walk, toss, roll my anxieties
Across the woeful phalanx of tedious waves,
Intermittently gorge my suffering
On a deceased lobster's tail,
Debate with petulance the meretricious merits
Of bay versus sea scallops
And like an indignant, jaded undertaker
Resuscitate then coddle my grievances,
Come beloved ambiguity,
Breed mystery and inscrutability
Into my absent, shrunken soul,
What tide would have me?
What yacht choose me for her earnest crew?
What destitute deception in sunsets
And salty, seditious waves am I called
To bear meaningless witness to?
Fraudulent skies like carnival barkers
Unfurl their palette of coastal tragedies,
Sailors flaunt their pennants and painters
Splatter artless miseries across resistant canvases,
I spread my pallid limbs like lifeless appendages
Along this scorching sand of unwelcome concupiscence,
We are volcanic islands adrift,
Perennially abused by the compelling,
Deceiving, distractions of a rancid,
Taunting, amoral nature,
I gorge once more on my lifeless crustacean

With reluctance and resignation,
Tolerate the requisite swim against my wishes,
Push a guileless child beneath the waves in jest,
Wait excitedly to welcome my sullen kin,
Hooded, cloaked and noxious night.

Wild Baby Gets Takeout

Wild Baby sat upon the sand
Fashioning his castle
With Wild Baby earnestness,
Yet building was a hassle,

Relentless waves grew in size,
Beat against his wall,
No sooner had he patted it
When it began to fall,

Yet in his heart Wild Baby knew
His fortress close to sea
Would in time erode away,
Soon would cease to be,

So with his soggy diaper low
Made up his mind to up and go
Get seafood takeout,

He raced across the scorching sand,
Taking orders as he went,
With seafood in such great demand
His task was heaven sent,

He jumped upon the counter,
Smiled from ear to ear,
In his best Wild Baby voice
Spoke for all to hear,

"I'll take 500 crab cakes,
200 lobster rolls,
10 gallons of clam chowder,

In huge, hot, heaping bowls,

50 plates of fish and chips
With scallops, rings, and fries,"
His order touched the diner's hearts,
Tears soon filled their eyes,

Fried clams, steamers, lots of slaw,
Tartar sauce in jugs,
Left the patrons all in awe,
Each gave Wild Baby hugs,

He topped it off with haddock,
A gigantic oyster plate,
1,000 calamari,
But it was getting late,

He reached the dunes
Above the beach,
Food balanced on his head,
Then, as we watched,
He tripped and fell,
Rolled down the dune instead,

His takeout burst upon the beach
As if from cannon shot,
Every single, tasty bit
Without exception caught,

They say if you were there that day
You had your fill of fish,
To feed his friends along the shore
Wild Baby's fondest wish.

Wild Baby & The Pirate

I blew a kiss, closed his door
Wild Baby breathed a sigh,
I'd wake him when
The morning sun
Revealed its golden eye,

No sooner had I closed the door,
Wild Baby slipped away,
Together with plush dinosaur
He'd gone to Cape Cod Bay,

He hung around the harbors there,
Black patch atop one eye,
Bandana tight across his curls,
He hailed a passerby,

"What is it mate?" the pirate said,
"You're much too young and plump,
I think that you belong in bed,
Say what's that on your rump?"

"You leave my diaper out of this,
You scurvy, swarthy creep,
I'd sooner sail the ocean sea
Than crawl in bed to sleep,"

"That's my boy," said he, said he,
And off they went to sea,
To plunder and to pillage
In riff-raff company,

They raided ports along the coast,
Kidnapped pirate girls,
Seduced by all his swagger,
Wild Baby's winsome curls,

They hung around with buccaneers,
Morgan, Silver, Kidd,
Rescued all those in distress,
At least Wild Baby did,

They boarded other sailing ships,
Wild Baby climbed the mast,
While brandishing a plastic sword,
A relic from his past,

He snacked upon some
Chocolate coins
That simulated gold,
Slept within a boson's chair,
At least that's what we're told,

I thought that we had lost him,
Becalmed or run aground,
But early one fine, sunny day,
This was what we found,

There within his trundle bed
Wild Baby snored away,
Upon his bed his pirate things
All now in disarray,

I whispered to his father,
"I told you he'd return,"
For pirates love their parents too
And while at sea they yearn
For home.

Wild Baby & The Whale

When last I spied our willful boy
He sat astride a whale,
Waved then headed out to sea,
And so begins this tale,
I sat up nights, paced the deck,
Asked the stars and moon
Where my bouncing baby was
To dissipate my gloom,
Our day had started
Blue and bright,
South Beach lay just ahead,
Wild Baby climbed upon the prow,
I feared he'd soon be dead,
But when the speeding runabout
Arrived on South Beach shores,
I recognized our little one,
The one with droopy drawers,
He sped ahead of all of us,
Wet diaper hanging low,
Signs that warned away from dunes
Suggested he should go,
He climbed upon the shifting mounds,
Slid down upon beach grass,
Bruised his fleshy arms and legs,
Scorched his tender bottom,
We set up camp quite near the surf
That rose and slammed ashore,
Delighted in the sun and sea
Alive with fish galore,

We strolled along the empty beach,
So white, so pure, so clean,
Asked a passing fisherman
If he perhaps he'd seen
Wild Baby,
Then we spied, just off the beach
Bobbing slowly by,
Within a pod of ocean seals,
Our smiling, little guy,
Paddling gaily with the pod,
Making not a fuss,
Without concern or even fear,
So far away from us,
That's when we saw the
Great white shark
Which trailed the tasty pack,
Just thinking of our wayward guy
We wished we had him back,
When suddenly a large, blue whale,
Largest in the sea,
Flipped Wild Baby on his back,
The rest is history,
Nightly then I paced the deck,
Where could Wild Baby be?
When last I looked, my headstrong boy
Was headed out to sea,
How he stayed atop the whale
A seacoast mystery,
One night, at last, I spotted him,

Fell full deep into a swoon,
For he was soundly sleeping
In the lap of the crescent moon,
Who winked at me with golden eye
And hummed a pleasant tune,
"I found your babe far out at sea,
The blue whale gave him back,
He took the risk and came with me,
You'll soon have what you lack,
When I descend to sea again
I'll hand him to the whale,
So will end your worries,"
So now ends this tale.

Mayflower At Peak Low Tide

Who would not have a merry heart?
What better way ones day to start?
Where else enchantment ever nigh?
Where else a more auspicious sky?
Where else an omnipresent god?
Where else a more resplendent sod?
Where else to witness boundless sea
Devoid of all duplicity?
What better place to loose ones soul,
Make one's tattered psyche whole,
Than here upon this fabled beach
Whose character none may impeach?

Whale Watch

The ship she dips and rises,
Green Gerty leans over the side,
The trawler she near capsizes,
Gerty knew she was in for a ride,
Her boat it lurches up and down,
Drops deep well into a trough,
While Gerty pleaded with her mates
To find her a way to get off,
She didn't listen to her gut,
Now her gorge complained,
Fresh blood that used to flood
Her face,
Now by the sea all drained.

Schooner Bar

It's only when he's lonely
That he comes and numbs,
Sits alone at the very end
Of the bar
Where the too tolerant tenders are,
A charming, fading, aging star,
Spit and polished older man,
Bright smile, white hair, golden tan,
Fine figure, often debonair,
With practiced, predatory eyes
Who soon another victim spies,
Pins him with compulsive talk
And a sad, desperate, interminable
Fusillade of words and stories,
All his faded glories,
His unwary victim, socially paralyzed,
Trapped in a barstool nightmare now,
Tenders hadn't warned him anyhow,
An older man's isolation without warning
Transmuted suddenly into aggression,
And if you heard his weekly confession
It's always late day loneliness,
Be kind, tactful, careful here,
He is your father, grandfather,
Brother, uncle, all dear,
And I fear may soon be me,
Invisible men you do not see.

Payne's Creek In Winter

To this day fair summer's charms
Payne's wintry vibrancy disarms,
At the far end of the John Wing Trail,
Expecting only cold travail,
I stepped upon encrusted sands
O'er laid with winter's harsh demands,
When, like a bolt, received a jolt
That put the lie to settled opinion,
Forever challenging summer's dominion
Over beauty, charm and coastal ecstasy,
Setting me free from a core belief
As summer thoughts now came to grief,
For here where creek and sea did meet,
Winter had prepared a rapturous treat
Of wind-whipped waves, bluest sky,
Ice bound marsh that seared the eye,
Sea drama, sounds, the crash of waves,
Aesthetics brazen winter saves
For the hardy and the tardy
Late to her splendor,
When in a flash each surrenders
To the midwinter melodrama here,
The sun, the surf, the sounds you hear,
Her all embracing, pure-sky air,
Sweet summer may not be as fair.

The Home We Lost

Why do we come?
Why do we sit and stare?
What are we waiting for?
We, the high strung, mischievous,
Liquid spawn of a liquid planet,
Lovingly nurtured by our mother
The sea, comprised of water,
Lighted salted just like mother,
Bioluminescent once, anxiety free once,
Except for the omnipresent predators,
Thrown up upon the land eons ago,
Abandoned, stranded, breathless,
Oppressed by gravity,
Now making curious, yearly pilgrimages
Back to mother,

Are we unhappy with the land?
Homesick? bored? unsettled?
Did evolution make a mistake,
By giving us arms, legs and curiosity?
Did we misplace something
We return each year to find?
The penniless buy shacks to look at her,
The rich build mansions to gaze,
Even the gulls stand and stare,
Haven't you wondered why?
I'll tell you why,

The sea tugs at you, will forever,
Until you grow back gills and fins
And one fine day endeavor
To merge with the watery home you lost
At such great cost.

Sunless Day

It was a sunless day
Yet not a cheerless one,
And though the sprightly me
Missed the sun,
I secretly craved such a day
And its low cloud cover,
Beneath which I
And sober thoughts
Might for a time pleasantly hover,
Which thoughts in sunshine are stillborn,
Or fly off into space,
How easy it is for sunny skies
To sober thoughts displace,
Yet by sober I don't mean to imply
Bad or sad,
For deeper, richer, profound thoughts
Will often make one glad,
So I sought out a roomy bluff,
A summit above the sea,
A height where I might probe and plumb
What deeper came to me,
And up they rose one by one,
As not a one would have done
Beneath a tranquilizing sun.

Watery Edge Of Life

Should I be getting ahead in the world
Or lying here on this beach lost to time?
Is self-acquaintanceship a crime?
Should I be efforting, striving,
Achieving more, wanting more,
Accepting that's what life is for?
Making others proud?
Declaiming what I do, where I live, out loud?
Acquiring reputation, fame, renown,
Making of my stardust soul
A blighted shantytown?
Getting ahead, but ahead of what?
Of whom? and why?

I see the results of anxious striving,
The cobbled together appearance of thriving,
The exorbitant price we all must pay
For "the good life" as they say,
Yet the older I get
The sillier seems that path
When I do life's simple math
And realize we lose the best
To end surfeited with all the rest,
Yet with my summer's new resolve,
Life's conundrum I will solve,
I will not care what others think,
At the watery edge of life I'll drink,
Counting the days I did not strive
As days when I was most alive.

Prayer For The Gifts Of The Sea

Grant me an open mind
Like to the spaciousness of this sea and sky,
Grant me steadfastness
Like to the tireless rhythms of this surf,
Grant me amiability
Like to the open-armed, welcoming beach itself,
Grant me tolerance
Like to the civility displayed by these bathers,
Grant me patience
Like to the slow, timeless work of nature here,
Grant me freedom from mind-created suffering
Like to the momentary enlightenment
I experience here,
Grant me self-possession
Like to the nobility of the creatures here,
Grant me a supple adaptability
Like to these malleable waters,
Grant me an intimate connection to the eternal
Like to the ineffable nexus I feel here,
Grant me a pervasive inner peace
Like to the preternatural calm that arises in me,
Whenever I visit these sandy, sacrosanct,
Inviolable precincts.

Provincetown At Dusk

Twilight, and the startled doe
Bolts from the tangled wood,
Lean, tawny muscles
Quick summoning speed
From where she stood,
In great, balletic bounds
She disappears into another
Leaving her fawn without a mother,

Her faun, still, unmoving,
Anxious, mute,
Quivering on shaky, untried legs,
Stared at us who'd caused the fuss,
We watched frozen
As the frightened faun retreated
The opposite way,
Deftly negotiating the thickets
In perfect little, lyrical leaps,
Nothing to say, dusk never keeps,
Night will fall, all will be well,
Nothing to learn, does return.

Before We Found Ourselves At Sea

Warm buttered toast, Earl Grey tea,
And a mound of pillows under me,
Lying abed night clothes on
Hours and hours beyond the dawn,
Newspapers, books piled high beside,
No one to comment, no one to chide,
Mind at peace, beach house at rest,
Expecting not a single guest,
A quiet corner, seashore view,
Psyche born today anew,
No place to go, no one to see,
Time to reacquaint with me,
Contented heart, sunlit room,
Anonymous my nom de plume,
This must be how it was meant to be
Before we found ourselves at sea,
I pull the covers over me.

Race Point Beach

I hear the faint footfalls of a giant,
Feel the near swales of pitch pine shudder,
Witness the proud, blonde dunes
Lower their sandy crowns in obeisance,
Sense the playful winds stand to,
Spy the agitated behemoths clustering
Off shore, churning the aqua sea
With slapping flukes and blowhole spray,
Soon realize not for us is their august display,
I witness too the powerful ocean
Taking note of their commotion
To modulate its surf and waves,

See how the newly-burnished sun
High waits upon the coming,
How the cerulean sky spreads wide its
Sapphire cloak and the broad, grassy
Beach, in deference,
Now slants to the briny deep,
So this nameless, seaborne god
Might her appointment keep,
I witness this vast coastal panorama
Now assume the very curve of the earth
Along its spreading, seafront girth,
A mighty goddess comes today,
No mortal should delay,
Come, away.

Sacred Rituals

Selection of a suit
With taste,
Stepping onto the sand
With an empty mind,
Choosing where to tan
With particularity,
Securing an umbrella
With fixity,
Placing a chair in the surf
With precision,
Flotation of the body
With the lightness of being,
Observing others
With discretion,
Emptying the cooler
With restraint,
Walking the beach
With no intent,
Combing the beach
With an eagle eye,
Reclining on the sand
With detachment,
Breaking of camp
With appreciation.

High Summer
Haiku

Alluring girl
In the surf,
Hope she's not
In love.

Shore creatures,
Why not vexed
Like us?

My lobster roll,
I suppress
Thoughts of sharing.

Long, empty beach,
Weighed down
By serenity.

One fully mindful
Beach day,
Vacation now over.

My eyes mist,
I count the summers
Left to us.

Residue of joy,
A coating of sand
In every room.

The loud family,
Teaches restraint
And detachment.

Self-conscious
In my suit,
Like everyone.

She slowly spreads
Her beach towel,
Many thoughts arise.

I swat a greenhead,
Hear
The Buddha weep.

I buy salt-water taffy,
Hear
My dentist chuckle.

I lose all inhibitions,
Must find them
By week's end.

Will your Heaven
Have beaches
Like these?

Whales gather
Offshore,
To people watch.

At night
I see the spaces
Left by fallen
Sea stars.

Corporate faces
In the water,
Children
Run to mother.

Joyful retriever
In the surf,
Seen through my
Inhibitions.

She disrobes,
The beach
Perceives a rival.

This placid beach,
Reminds how noisy
The mind is.

The Creator is present,
Don't ask
How I know.

Private beach sign,
Fear and defiance
Arise in the walkers.

The public,
In all shapes and sizes,
Stirs a summer compassion.

The image of your absent face,
Settles over the beach,
To the left,
To the right.

A nearby gull,
Models discretion
And personal space.

Groaning cooler,
Dragged by the most
Ample bather.

Beach bodies,
How differently
Men and women
Are constructed.

A Writer's Room

I'm looking for a small, charming, modest room,
An aspiring writer's room,
Something snug, sunny, half-hidden and high
That instantly catches a writer's eye,
A dreamer's room reserved for constructing
A temple of silence, tinged with romance,
Near to nature, farther from man,
With a clear open view of the night sky,
And there are so many to chose from here,
A veritable myriad of writer's rooms
On the Cape & Islands:
Lofty cupola with four way views
And full, dazzling daylight,
Pinnacle room in a Victorian turret,
Bay window room that looks
Upon an infinite, lime green marsh,
Cozy keeper's room atop a lighthouse,
A room just below a widow's walk,
Refinished barn set back in a wildflower meadow,
An attic room with its own balcony,
A bay window room fronting the sea,
An aging outbuilding behind a sea captain's home,
A one-room dune shack,
The highest room in that inn,
A room at the far end of a greenhouse,
A saltbox off to the back and side,
An alcove, a shed, a gazebo, a shanty,
A garret, a bungalow, a cottage, a shack,
Something delightful, something cozy,

Something to summon the Muses back,
I'm looking for a writer's room,
Do you have one for me
And my ethereal friends?
If you do and I ask if we might have a view,
Please let us in, so we may admire,
Invoke, and imagine.

Taboo On The Beach

There is a certain topic ever present in the mind,
Not a soul will raise it, no mention will you find,
It courses through the old and young, all those in between,
Conceals itself within the mind reluctant to be seen,
No bathers will refer to it, taboo on the beach,
Yet just behind the eyes and mind remains within your reach,
Muscles out all other thoughts, compelling, urgent, brash,
Lurks and hides behind a mask, intrudes within a flash,
Distressing, far too personal, too potent by a mile,
More inclined to raise a brow than others to beguile,
Has no place upon the sand with children, families near,
Would shock, alarm, unnerve, distract, instill a primal fear,
Yet there it is, full front of mind, amidst the tanning throng,
To speak of day jobs on a beach is almost always wrong.

School Of The Shore

To know presence
Notice what your senses sense,
To know unselfconsciousness
Observe young children,
To know restraint
Watch others consume,
To know patience
Wait for the clouds to pass,
To know fidelity
Take counsel from the tides,
To know boundaries
Spread your towel
Near a beauty,
To know compassion
Suspend all judgment,
To know tolerance
Come at midday,
To know joy
Float with your eyes closed,
To know humility
Don a bathing suit,
To know life balance
Notice the harmony
Of sea, sand and sky,
To know self-possession
Observe the creatures,
To know wisdom

Do a kindness, then another,
To know the meaning of life
Open your eyes.

Scusset On The Fourth

Round the bay mute sparklers fly
Against a pitch and spangled sky,
Round one great curve they rise, they fall,
Soundless, joyous, fireworks all,
Fleeting flashes far away
Illuminating Cape Cod Bay,
The fact that you can't hear them
Seems to endear them even more
To those who know what freedom's for,
From Herring Cove to Ryder's,
Kingsbury to Howe's,
Cross Sandy Neck to Scusset Beach
As line of sight allows,
Yet as the distant show abates
A chill sweeps off the sea,
I wonder have we done enough
To keep our nation free?

Shelly And Whiskers

A likeable loggerhead named Shelly,
Away off shore upon his belly,
Spied a giant monster there,
Whiskered with great size to spare,
"Who might you be?" asked young Shelly
"With your massive, slate grey belly?"
"Who is asking?" said the seal
Intent his true name to conceal,
"I am asking," said our turtle
"Watch me now your belly hurtle,"
Then before he could reply,
In the blink of a sea turtle's eye,
Shelly leaped his great, gray span,
Our startled Whiskers overran,

"My name is Whiskers, if you please,
You needn't vault my span to tease,
I'd like to be your friend and swim,
Dive and feed upon a whim,
I am a harbor seal you see, quite cute,
Unshaven as can be,
If you would keep your eye on me
I'd keep an eye on you,
We could swim the days away,
Take in all the view,"

Smiling Shelly raised his flipper
And now feeling mighty chipper,
Pointed both of them to shore
Where our coast they might explore,
So if you spy a loggerhead
Cavorting with a seal,
Do not mistrust your eyes my friend,
Such things are no big deal.

Shorebirds

Four Short-Billed Dowagers, Three Common Nightwalkers,
Nine Bare Breasted Wobblers, One Black Crowned Night Heroine,
One Virginia Reel, Six Blue Heroines, Fifteen Northern Hurriers,
Forty Breeding Teenagers, Five Piping Hot Lovers,
One Good Tern then another, Twelve Northern Snow Shovelers,
Six Bobbleheads, Eight Mute Swains, Several Old Coots,
Five Parasitic Joggers, Twenty Mating Pairs,
Five Red-Necked Peasants, Two Ruddy Turncoats,
Five Greater Tanned Yellowlegs, Four Lesser Tanned Yellowlegs,
One Ascetic Monk Paraclete, Three Yellow-Bellied Suckers,
Six Common Cravens, One Yellow Rumped Wobbler,
Two Well Done Ovenbirds, Seven Full Breasted Starlets,
Twenty-two Mitered Cardinals. One Red Necked Plebe,
One Matte Ibis, One Glossy Ibis,
One Brant Light, One Laconic Swan, One Voluble Swan,
Six Eurasian Wedgies, One American Wedgie,
One Surf Scooter, Three Beach Kites, One Comb Over Eagle,
A Sharp-Shinned Gawker, Two Cheeky British Petrols,
One Ring Fingered Duck, One Broad Minded Hawk,
One Roughed Up Grouch, Six Pot Bellied Lovers,
One Bare Breasted Sandpiper, Three Long Tailed Joggers,
Four Stone Skimmers, One Dazed Kingfisher,
Two Yellow Bellied Slackers, One Thick Lipped Starlet,
One Topless Nuthatch, One Full Rumped Starlet,
One Tennessee Wobbler, Two Wild Turkey Wobblers,
Two Uncrowned Kinglets, One Snow and one Flag Bunting,
Two Snail Mail Crossbills, One Six Pack Pectoral Sandpiper,
Spotted Sandpiper, then spotted another,
One Monk Parakeet with two Northern Cardinals.

South Beach Chatham

Hurling furious, frightful waves
She paws with foamy hands,
As far as the sharpest eye can see
To the north and southern lands,
Her curving shoreline all in white
Contrasts with her cobalt blue,
As wave after formidable wave
Agitates the vast sea view,
She's angry, threatening, potent,
Pounding her fists on the sand,
Demanding constant attention
With her back-beat, percussive band,
Yet for all her relentless bellowing,
Churn of spindrift mist,
Her cannonade becomes white noise
The more she appears to insist,
Like a narcotic, her salt sea air
Flows into my nostrils and chest,
Imperturbable gulls bob on her back,
I sense she is due for a rest,
I retreat to a cleft in a nearby dune
To wait out her daunting display,
And know in the quiet of my lair
That I was alive today.

Winter Wind At Red River Beach

Late one night within my room
I heard the fierce wind blow,
It wrapped itself around my house
Made a mighty show,
Pounded on my window panes
As if to let me know
That it was king and
Not the ice and snow,
Kept me from my deepest sleep,
Unnerved me at the first,
When from my long unsettled mind
This deeper question burst,
Winter wind, say winter wind,
Are you an indifferent wind?
Is there meaning in your blast?
With some intent were you precast?
The winter wind blew for a time,
Sighed, with deep composure
Then replied,
Don't flatter yourself, do not fear
Just because my wind is near,
It's not about you,
Neither am I indifferent too,
I know nothing of philosophy,
You'll get no insight here from me,
I'm just the wind and nothing more,
Go and latch your cottage door,
Of frigid blasts I have yet more,
I only know what wind is for,

I pulled my blanket over me,
Dispensed with night philosophy,
Realized then I might have sinned
For it was just the winter wind.

Still Life

Red rowboat leaning against
A shingled shack,
Multi-colored lobster buoys
Free climbing a barn wall,
Fan shaped scallop shells
Lovingly spaced along a sill,
Translucent sea glass
Catching morning light
In a bay window,
Miniature lighthouses
In a favorite nook,
Lobster traps neatly stacked
On a town fish pier,
Plush whales waiting
In a child's bedroom,
Brass anchors just so
Upon a wall,
Surf casting rods upright
In the sand,
Hand carved ships
Along a mantle,
Blue Hydrangea blooms
On a bedside table,
Little here is motion
And I have a notion
For a life as still,
For the peace of shells
Upon a sill.

True Blue

This sand will not disown me,
This sea will not betray,
This sun presents a single face,
No Janus-faced display,

These waves will soothe
When times are tough,
This breeze when others go,
This beach is never envious,
Like some false friends I know,

This coast is ever guileless,
Stalwart, fair, true blue,
Like my beagle, wags its tale,
Will do the same for you.

We Foul Our Air And Sea

Has anybody noticed
We're a reckless race?
Has anyone stopped to think
About our frantic pace?
Has anyone considered
We foul our air and sea,
Without whose generous bounty
We likely wouldn't be?
Has anyone you know observed
We bump each other off,
With guns, with knives,
In cars, in wars,
In planes we fly aloft?
Has anyone yet pointed out
How we treat the beasts?
We either hunt them
Till they're gone
Or make of them a feast,
Has anybody mentioned
We form our little group,
Set about to demonize,
Knock theirs for a loop?
Has anybody noted
We seem an anxious lot,
Confusing those who made us,
What is it they forgot?

The kindest thing we could do
If aliens should land,
Would be to urge them
All to shoo
In gentle reprimand.

Rock Harbor Beach

At Rock Harbor Beach far out on the Cape,
Word got around mighty fast,
The sun was setting right over the bay,
Its painterly sky wouldn't last.

So the sanderlings, rails, gannets and gulls
Settled down on the narrow town beach,
Staked out a bit of attractive terrain
While keeping the sun within reach,

To join in the fun blue crabs came ashore,
Angling along with much clatter,
When dozens of dolphins
Beached themselves,
The lack of saltwater no matter,

Jellyfish came but stayed offshore,
(Little room was left on the sand,)
Excited by rumors they'd heard in the sea
Concerning the famous town band,

A hush soon settled over the scene,
Cloud curtains drew back in the sky,
The sun proudly preened right over the bay
To the sighs of the whales swimming by,

That day, it is said, if you stayed in your bed,
You missed the best sunset of all,
Don't miss the next and go to bed vexed,
Come heed the loud Kittiwake's call.

Frost In Falmouth

Whose beach this is I think I know,
I pray the owner doesn't show,
She would not like me stopping here
To stroll her beach, dip my toe,

My little hound must think it queer
To trespass with her sign so near,
Beyond the public beach and sand,
Sunniest morning of the year,

He gives his soggy coat a shake,
Does a canine double take,
The only other sound's the roar
Of foamy surf and wavy break,

Her private beach is broad, unique,
But I have yet another week,
And miles to go of hide and seek,
And miles to go of hide and seek.

Tan Lines

Tan Lines

Who knew that I would find myself
At last by finding you?
Who knew that I would trade my life
For one pure heart that's true?
Who knew that my constricted heart
Would glide upon the air?
Who knew that tanning on this beach
Was such a one so fair?
Who knew that handsome beaches
Could engineer a match,
Or such a roving, restless heart
So easily dispatch?

Skip A Stone

Skip a stone for romance,
Skip a stone for love,
Skip a stone to nudge the fates
You're at the mercy of,
Skip a stone to make a wish,
Skip a stone for luck,
Skip a stone to get your life
From stasis to unstuck,
Skip a stone for love that's fierce,
Blazing, bold and new,
Skip a stone to find a mate
With eyes for only you,
Find a perfect heart-shaped stone,
Close your eyes and say,
Dance upon this water stone,
Bring true love my way.

This Is New England

A perceptible, sensual energy
Falls like a fine mist,
Settles over the teeming beach
Like a fairy dust,
Adding something dangerous,
Inflammatory, unsettling,
And quite lovely
To the soft sand,
But this is New England
My curious friend,
It's more
Than we can stand.

The Bard On The Beach

Once more onto the beach dear friends,
Once more or button up this coast
With our sweet, high summer days all spent,
At work there's nothing so becomes a man
As feigned obsequiousness, prudent restraint,
But when the beckoning breezes
Sound in the ears, then mimic
The seductions of the satyr,
Trim the untaut, tumid flesh, summon up the stud,
Conceal stark nature with a flattering suit,
Freely fix your roving eyes in wild pursuit,
I see you stand like eager lovers in the high dunes,
Straining upon the heart, bare of foot,
Come gents, follow your passions,
And upon my fervent imperative cry,
For romance, summer, Cape & Islands!

Cape Rap #2

By the sea, you and me,
All that wonder there for free,
For us to take and shake off the city,
Would be a pity, if all that pretty
Goes to waste and we never get to taste
Salt sea air, lose a care,
Find us there, time to spare,
Time to chill, with a will,
Come with me girl, take a whirl,
Take a chance to enhance our mood, soul food,
Cool dude, elude, take a splash, swim and play,
What's that you say? any ole way? take my hand
On the sand, unplanned, who's in command?
See the sky, by and by, chase the gulls,
Watch 'em fly, right on by, what's your reply?

You kiddin' me, trickin' me, can't you see I wanna be
By your side, in the tide, swimmin' free,
You and me, salt sea air, no compare, take me there,
Only fair, time to spare, no more care,
Got my suit, got my hat, you're all that,
Don't be so insular, go find me that peninsula,
Show me a whale, tell me a tale, while we sail,
Eat a full-bellied clam, here I am,
This ain't no cryptogram, no anagram, damn.

Affaire De Coeur

Is our summer bond a breach of faith?
Evidence of disloyalty? are we cheating?
Is our yearly seaside romance self-defeating?
I know it looks bad to the wider world,
When I admit to loving you
With such outrageous passion as I do,
When I celebrate our seaside
Intimacies to all who care to hear,
Is it perfidy, marital betrayal even,
If year-to-year I never fail
To seek you out?
Dream of you each night,
With far too secretive delight?

I care not what the world may think,
Come summer I shall once again sink
Into your amorous, aqueous arms,
And with surpassing joy
Garland my lovesick head
With your ornamental seaweeds,
Dive, splash, float and play,
Gladly give my pledged heart away,
Each and every summer day.

Bayside Bliss

A stellar sigh, stolen kiss,
Fleeting taste of bayside bliss,
Then a miss,

And for each a deep abyss,
What's worse for callow hearts
Than this?

Lifetime to reminisce,
Upon a sigh, upon a kiss.

Was That Good For You

On an incomparable beach day
Round mid-high tide,
With an onshore, beckoning breeze,
A broad smiling, angled sun,
The ocean clear, crisp and clean,
With just the right invigorating chill,
Comely little wavelets
Small enough to tame,
Yet large enough to play with,
And a congenial, vacant mind,
Free, uncluttered, brim full
Of childlike expectation,
The very first ocean swim
Of the summer season
Beats intimacy hands down,
For every woman on the beach
And one centenarian male.

Figment

There was a man made ardent love
To women on the beach,
Yet not a soul could point him out,
He seemed beyond their reach,
He left no footprints on the sand,
No evidence to trace and
Not one female could describe
The features of his face,
He never introduced himself,
Begged them shed their clothes,
Lured them to this sandy shore
Or set them all in rows,
No charm was his, nor gifts, nor looks,
He never laid a hand,
Unlike normal fiends and crooks
On sea, in air, or land,
Every single male was quizzed,
Each in turn denied,
Yet every single woman thought
That each in turn had lied.

While Summer Lingers Near

I chase you and you run away,
I stop, you stop the same,
I walk away, you follow me,
Is summer love a game?
I wander in its labyrinth,
Uncertain, ardent, meek,
While you, aloof and lofty,
Seldom deign to speak,
You permeate my soul again,
I climb back in the ring,
A devotee of pain and loss,
A worthless, pining thing,
You smile a fleeting, saucy smile,
Beckon me to come,
I purge myself of daily doubt
Your rarities to plumb,
What strange insanity
Is this, so captivating me,
That has me its potent grip
Right up against the sea?
I cannot stop or save myself,
You too are tethered here,
Our fates requires we two dance
While summer lingers near.

Morning At Howe's

I must to the beach, I must to the sea,
I must to my waking beauty,
More than a daily chore, my friend,
An existential duty,

I must to the hill that guards her,
I must to the trodden dune,
The sea grass rise that guards her well
This temperate morn in June,

I must to the call of lowest tide,
I must to the barren mile,
I must to her broad expanse of sand,
Her lovely, long profile,

I must to the early morning treat
Of a swim in her cooling plumes,
I must to her gorgeous silences
Before the midday blooms,

I must to her soaring gulls and terns,
I must to her sun above,
I must to the one who waits for me there,
My only other love.

Come Sweet Girl

Come, sweet girl, to the edge of the sea
Where the blue hydrangeas bloom,
Come, my love, along with me
For within my heart there's room
For another love as fine as you,
Another just as fair and
That is the shore that calls to me,
I will take you there,

If I must share your love, dear boy,
If I must settle for less,
I have to admit I feel the same,
I here to you confess,
We'll each make room
In our hearts for the shore,
For the silken sand and the sea,
There's room in our hearts
For more than two, but please
No more than three.

Hazy As It Is

Many years ago while beach walking
With my new, young wife,
On a sudden, thoughtless whim
I swam out vigorously,
Apparently too enthusiastically,
To recover a blue, white,
And red-striped beach ball,
Which I repatriated by hand
To a very appreciative young woman
In a barely-there, electric orange bikini,
String tied loosely on each side,
Five foot seven or so she was,
With admirable posture, a flirty demeanor,
Long, auburn hair with streaks of blonde,
Sparkling hazel eyes, a taut dancer's body,
A broad, gap-toothed smile
That suggested far too much,
And a figure that commanded the tides,
Just then in full obeisance,
I'm reminded of that harrowing event often,
Yet my memory of it, hazy as it is,
Brings to me, even today, a secret joy
And a vital burst of long spent youth.

Time Is A Runner

I want to hold you,
Why?
You know why,
For how long?
Forever,
We just met,
I know,
Seems too soon,
Maybe so, but
Time is a runner,
Is that all you want?
No,
What else?
Never mind,
Tell me,
I want to build you
A Cape cottage
With a pitched roof,
End gables
And a fine stone wall,
Live with you by the pounding sea,
Drink strong Irish tea,
Bounce your babies on my knee,
Come hold me then,
Now?
Yes, tighter,
Why?
Time is a runner.

Which Did The Rains Reprove

A nice young fella
With a small umbrella
And a cute girl by his side,
Came down the beach,
Set up two chairs and
With her watched the tide,
The sky grew fearsome,
Thunder came,
All other bathers left,
Lightning flashed to their right,
Then just to their left,
Soon the rains began to fall
And with a clever move,
He popped a brelly overhead
Which did the rains reprove,
Lifeguards urged them both to leave,
They smiled and each declined,
Since that day their image has
For me true love defined.

A Very Articulate Hound

Dogs will only speak with you when no one else is there,
Every owner knows it's true, they're much too shy to share,

I took my beagle for a walk along a nearby beach,
What happened next is true, I swear, has so much to teach,

I walked along at even pace, he cantered proudly near,
Paraded like he owned the beach, put other dogs in fear,

We walked perhaps a mile or more when up ahead we saw
A comely girl with her own dog, she without a flaw,

We walked the route we always did, she did the very same,
My Rusty was uneasy, until at last we came
To a decision,

Do we follow close behind or walk the other way?
She might assume we're following, intending to waylay,

"We must not follow close behind," is what my Rusty said,
In a most distinguished, British voice with lowered, sniffing head,

"I will not change our normal route," I told him, quite surprised,
I saw he didn't buy my thought, he turned and locked my eyes,

"You're married, she is likely too, that should quite inhibit you,
You cannot fool this beagle, Jack, with you I go a long way back,"

"I think you're wrong," I told him straight, we went the other way,
We haven't seen that pretty girl to this very day,

Dogs will only talk to you with no one else around,
At times I owe my marital bliss to a very articulate hound.

With Poise And Perfect Grace

The shore today's attended by a servile sun,
Whose brightly beaming presence
Once more she has clear won,
By tame and temperate breezes
Here today as well,
As though she holds all nature
Once more within her spell,
So too the tides that flood her sands
As though they sprint to heed commands,
Sensed by nature here arrayed,
So that the preening, prideful shore
To best advantage is once again displayed,

Yet I some mischief have prepared for her,
To startle obsequious nature, cause a littoral stir,
And you my love shall play a role today,
So ever after all who visit here will say:
One day, in ages past, I witnessed here
The only time this shore beheld a peer,
And so displayed an envy sensed by all,
The day a young man's lover came to call,
Who sunned herself with poise and perfect grace
And for a time all coastal charms
Did utterly displace.

Along The Sounding Sea

One day along the sounding sea
A solitary called to me
By a name I used to be,
The indifferent look upon my face
Arrested his ambitious pace,
Averting his eyes he quietly passed
As if he had not even asked,

I resumed my stroll as well,
Disinclined to ever tell
I might have answered to that name
Long ago before you came,
Yet like this margin of sand and sea
We merged my love and ceased to be
What each had been in individuality,

That day along the sounding sea
I was happy I had ceased to be,
For you were long a part of me
And I of you,
If ever my name is called again
As it was that blustery day,
I'll happily feign indifference then,
Continue on my fated way
From me to you.

There Was A Lissome Mommy

There was a lissome mommy
Sunbathing by the sea,
She had a bawling babe with her
Who gurgled, cooed at me,

I mentioned that she had a burn,
She rose and looked to see,
Though she put more lotion on,
She still looked hot to me.

Beach House

My beach house sits atop a rise
Just above the sea,
It has a view of shoreline
Where I will live with thee,
It has three bowed bay windows
Wide to out of doors,
Turrets, writer's cupola,
Knotty pinewood floors,
Fronted by a grassy dune,
Fine pathway to the beach,
From nor'easters well immune
That won't our joy impeach,
With lots of little porches,
Many darling decks,
A rooftop walk, a waterfall,
So many fine aspects,
Built in shelves
For well-bound books,
Half hidden hideaways,
Lots of comfy, nestled nooks,
For chilly, rainy days,
Neighbors too beyond our view
Yet not beyond our hearts,
For whether they be old or new
Friends go in fits and starts,
A beach house with amenities
Seems wonderful and fun,
Yet my heart reminds me dear
Our beach house needs but one.

A Sailor Climbed The Mizzenmast

A sailor climbed the mizzenmast,
Another furled the sails,
A third was lazy, drunk and bored,
Therein lies our tale,

The third soon spied the captain's wife,
Oh boy was she a prize,
She sunned herself upon the deck,
Did there delight his eyes,

He doffed his suit and like a brute
Lay down right beside her,
The captain spied the two of them
But he was not a fighter,

A sailor climbs the mizzenmast,
A second furls the sails,
The third tans with the captain's wife
Quaffing stouts and ales.

Ingénue

I come to the beach
To be with friends,
Have some fun, share the sun,
Gossip, laugh, pass the time,
I come to the beach
To let my budding body
Move in all the healthy ways
A beach invites,
I come to the beach
Innocent and free,
Yet feel your eyes on me,

I sense something else now too,
Something quickening,
Something for later,
When I am ready to be
Where you are now,
When nature timely tells me so,
Gives a proper nudge,
Encourages me to go,
But for now I'll it be,
And yet, and yet,
I feel your eyes on me.

Catch Of The Day

From far away I watched her
Retriever bounding time and again
Into the surging surf,
Freer than a sunbather,
Full of animal energy,
Muscular, sodden, gilded coat
Aglint in the noonday sun,
Quick paddling a succession of
Waves to retrieve a ball,
Then obediently dropping it
At her feet,

When she, with a thin,
Strong right arm
And a charming, girly motion,
Threw it again, and then,
As if no one else was on the sand,
Laughed repeatedly to herself,
As the wind played with
Her long, dark hair and she
With all my thoughts,

At that moment she seduced
My wandering eyes,
Arrested my beach walk,
Quieted the stentorian sea,
Emptied the shore
Of all other bathers,
Made the broad sky sullen and
Easily routed the admiring sun
Into a quick retreat,

Tall and lithe she was
With a beautiful face,
Frolicking there,
Wearing but a tan,
Kissed summer long
By admiring beams and so entered
The catalogue of beauty
In my dreams,

When her golden, at the behest of
Some mischievous god's silent
Imperative, dropped the ball
Right at my feet,

I tossed it underhand to her
With an approving, too-broad smile,
And as it sailed
In a slow motion, interminable arc,
Her green eyes rose
To track its aerial progression,
And my own eagerly left
Their dwelling place,

My agitated heart
Riveted me to the spot
As the envious sea
Increased its roar,
The annoyed sun intensified his
Glare and the now jealous clouds
Proud puffed their chests,

She caught it one handed,
I caught her glance with two,
Then reluctantly moved
Along the beneficent sand,
Turning now and again
To hear her fading laughter,

The restive sea is a restorative,
As is a gentle sun, so too
Are all those creatures
Who make the tame blood run.

Corn Hill Beach

First impressions deceive here too,
As her constant motion
Belies her claim to calm,
As her distant clouds puff, rise,
And, in slow transit,
Trek unnoticed along the far horizon,
As her colossal comers roll in,
Then the sea itself, then all out again,
As onshore breezes sculpt her dunes,
Bend and sway her sea grasses,
As her avian creatures rise, glide,
And slow-swooping, fall,
As her hidden fishes dart about
As solitary truants,
Or clustered in their schools,
As her basking bathers hug the dunes,
Then en masse migrate to the sea,
Then back again, by and by,
When the rising tide is high,
As her vessels crisscross her waters,
As her umbrella's flutter
And reclining voices mutter
Across her soothing sands,
Yet my love you needn't fear,
Not everything's inconstant here,
Some static things well out of view,
Like my unbending thoughts of you.

When I Was A Child

When I was a child these waves were wild,
This sky was windy and clear,
I came to the beach with a magical mind,
Fancy and dreamtime were near,

Now I am a man, these waves are tame,
This sky now sullen and drear,
Clouds that pass in a somber sequence
Form a face that occasions a tear.

Smitten With The Sea

Say I am smitten with the sea
If ever they should question thee,
Her sensuous amplitude,
Endless catalogue of charms,
Wind that roars, then becalms,
Her wild tumult, deeper blues,
Fine pastels, softer hues,
Her aloof passivity, perverse proclivity
In stormy squall to frighten all,
Her nurturing depths
Where creatures play,
Deeper down where fades
The lyrical light of day,
Her drama, moods, vocal choice,
Her baritone, soprano voice,
Her labyrinthine depths, synchronous tides,
Lovely, sea green, mermaid brides,
She never disappoints,
Meets me on the wonted path
With fine display of joy or wrath,
Most often in June
Beneath a sculpted, beach grass dune,
It is the sea I love the most,
From this captivating coast
To warmer climes,
And it seems to me at times
That I fell first,
That my youthful heart did fairly burst

When first we met,
So if, my love, someone should say
Why is his look so far away?
Tell them, though he lies with me,
He is still smitten with the sea.

Dream On

What if you, one day, spotted
The most alluring woman
In the surf,
Found sufficient courage,
And with manly resolve stood,
Chin up, stomach in, shoulders back,
And calmly approached her
With a large, dry beach towel
As she emerged from the sea
Dripping wet from her swim?
What if you smiled at her,
Complimented her on her looks,
Her unimpeachable loveliness,
Gently brushed her wet hair back,
Kissed her chastely on her shapely neck,
Embraced her like in the movies,
Long enough not to be inappropriate
Yet long enough to get your point across?
What if she was most appreciative,
Kindly asked your name, then
Asked if she might join you on the sand?
Wouldn't that be something?
Dream on, fantast.

Boundaries On The Beach

Where is the line
One dare not cross,
That may, one day,
Cause each a loss?
That gauzy line 'tween
Flirt and fault, o'er which
Unguarded hearts may vault?
I asked myself, no answer got,
Seeking it still, my summer lot,

So appealing she was that day
With rare, exquisite charm,
Rich dark hair,
Slender leg and arm,
So enticing she was that day
With little to say,
Tanning the dreamy day away,
Alone, as was I,

She was a calamity that day,
Causing much disquiet,
The slumbering hearts
Insurgent riot,
Bound and available,
Tied yet free,
Onset of profound
Affliction for me,

Our brief chat was a
Pitched battle,
Her words, now indistinct
In the mind,
Still sound within the heart,
Tension of the lethal kind,

She was circumspect, on guard,
Yet found it not too hard
To stay and listen
To my awkward, tumbling,
Ill chosen words,
Against which a married woman girds
For self protection,
Words spoken much too fast
From one so desperate
To make a sunny moment last,

She is a naughty truant now,
And I, bound yet free,
Still keep my vow,
Yet ask myself even now:
Where is the line
One dare not cross,
That may, one day,
Cause each a loss?

By The Sea

Women who would never show
Parts that set men's eyes aglow,
Put every charm within the reach
Of strangers on a sunny beach,
A glance that merits piercing looks,
Dangling males on tenterhooks,
At work or on a train,
Seems most welcome on the shore
As she doffs, parades and more,
Perhaps she thinks she is at home,
That I am her mate,
For as she jettisons her clothes
She does not hesitate,
Nor it seems does public space
Inhibit her intent,
Though my towel mates with hers
She voices no dissent,
She blithely shows her features
To curious and sundry creatures,
Her every fetching curve and hill
Conveys a silent thrill along the sand,
Where every male's imagination
Is now at her command,
Young men compelled by blood to act
Soon forfeit all their peace,
While older males just gaze and smile,
Age grants well earned release,

I now know all their lovers know
Save for touch and voice,
As yearly I will look and smile
And by the sea rejoice.

Ever The Same

What first appears
A changeless place,
Serene, calm, ever the same,
For our questing human race
Merits another name: mutable shore,
From its protean dunes
To the torsion of its waves,
From its jetsam strewn
To its bird conclaves,
From its moody sky
That puts the lie
To an even disposition,
To the shifting cadence of its surf
That seems an imposition
To one counting on the legato
Of its ambient music,
From its sudden squalls
To the variable calls
Of its shorebirds,
From the booming ordnance
Of a nascent storm
To its air that morphs
From chill to warm,
From the restless creatures of its deep
That never sleep, never sleep,
To its changing colors, variable hues,
That suddenly morph
From greens to blues,
Though I understand

Sea and sky heed no command
To remain the same,
My love goes by another name,
So fixed, so constant,
Ever the same.

First Encounter Beach

A pilgrim came, moored nearby,
Her shallop was a jeep,
Young and lithe, fair to the eye,
No words had I to speak,
She lugged her things across the sand,
Settled near to me,
Spread her towel, set her chair
Full up against the sea,
The day was flat until she came,
My thoughts mundane and bland,
Yet now a breath of cleansing air
Blew clear across the sand,
The sea which I had doted on,
The breaking surf, the sky,
No longer held my interest,
A rival sunned nearby,
Uncanny how a lovely girl
Will turn the mind around,
Rout all other random thoughts,
Every man confound,
I tried to read, I tried to swim,
I tried my best to focus, yet
All attempts in vain that day,
She had such hocus pocus,
Until the moment when her hat,
Uplifted by a breeze,
Gave to me a single chance
I did not fail to seize,
She stood, she smiled,

She whispered thanks
There at the edge of the sea,
It was our first encounter,
Yet not the last for me.

My Favorite Beach

My favorite beach is a masterpiece
Of heavenly handiwork,
Lying tranquil against a broad bay,
Promising peace and rich rejuvenation,
Welcoming me unconditionally,
Flooding my parched soul
With unearned grace,
Offering languor and a myriad
Of minor pleasures,
Lifting the sullen spirit to soar,
Opening like a blossom to the amiable sun,
Bubbling in the mind like Veuve Clicquot,
Conflating sea, sand and sky
In miraculous shades of blue,
Gentling the aqua surf,
Dispersing buoyant bathers
Along its luxurious, languid length,
Softening the spirit like an emollient,
Summoning my lover's intoxicating smile,
Carrying her sweet bouquet
Upon its soothing currents of air,
For me alone to respire,
For me alone to savor.

Dark Magic

Swimming at night to the erotic delight
Of the other in the coal-black pitch,
Guided to water's edge by sound only,
Swiftly dispensing with suits,
Oblivious to subterranean dangers,
The entire natural world holding itself
In rapt abeyance,
Suspended for the length of our embrace,
Assuming a vigilant voyeurism
For the brief duration
Of our skinny dip and dalliance,
I remember the night, the fright,
The carnal delight,
Yet I do not remember her name.

The Dance

Pay more attention to the dance,
What beach life's all about,
Don't spend all your time tanning,
Daydreaming, reading, beachcombing,
Pay attention to the dance,
The mating dance,
Primal, visceral, all around you,
These bathers, all bipedal, hairless primates,
All nearly naked, exchanging pheromones,
Flaunting body parts,
Displaying barely hidden charms,
Observe like an anthropologist,
See the beach through a new lens,
A lens suffused with sensual excess,
Unacknowledged, largely unconscious,
Yet palpable as the sand you lie upon,
Notice the preening,
The signaling, the sideways glances,
Displays of virility and femininity,
This isn't a beach at all,
It's an unrestrained, National Geographic
Watering hole orgy of animal excess,
And you're an intimate part of it,
A nearly nude, uninhibited drama
Worthy of Herculaneum and Pompeii,
Pay more attention to the dance,
Everyone, including you,
Is in their underpants.

Baby Beach Bermuda

Where are you, Jack?
Why do you ask?
I have a funny feeling,
About what?
You're not cheating on me, are you, Jack?
Nope,
Why do I feel this way then?
No idea,
Tell me where you are, Jack,
Right now?
Yes, Jack,
If you must know, I'm at Baby Beach,
But Jack?
What?
There's no such beach on the Cape & islands.
I spoke with Martha and Nan,
They confirmed it,
Look, there's no need to feel hurt,
You want me
To see the world, don't you?
But another beach? really Jack?
If I don't try other beaches, how can I
Appreciate the eminence of yours?
Besides, it's only research to confirm
What everyone knows,
You know I don't like sophistry, Jack,
Never did,
I know, but it's true, kind of,
Enjoy Bermuda, Jack,
Watch for the undertow.

Wooden Boat

Our wooden boat is not a yacht
With fancy trim and sail,
There are some things I have forgot
While building on a smaller scale,
It has no copper rivets,
No decks with teakwood laid,
Yet all its planks and fittings
With you in mind were made,
It does not have a custom hull
Or laminated spars, yet
Unlike larger wooden boats
This little craft is ours,
It has no cross-planked bottom
Or polished, bronze stern light,
Yet with its open canopy
We'll see the stars at night,
It has two rowing stations,
Small cooler 'neath our feet,
Two finely crafted, sturdy oars,
For each a window seat,
We'll row our boat
Quite close to shore,
Take no crew along,
Find secluded, covert coves,
Sing a sailor's song,
For all our rowboat's missing
In rigging, sails, and size,
Like you, our little wooden boat
Is lovely on the eyes.

Goldfish

I only want to lie here
On this soothing sand,
Beneath this rainbow
Beach umbrella, eating
Cheddar baked goldfish
With you,

I don't want to commute,
Self promote, curry favor,
Climb the ladder, blend in,
Toe the line, self-censor,
Be reviewed, be spoken to,
Strive to impress, kowtow,
Align with the norm, be savvy,
Own things for others to admire,
Prove myself, run faster,
Amount to something,
Defer my dreams, fit in,
Exceed expectations,
Play the game, network,
Become well spoken,
Adopt others values,
Or pretend that appearance
Is everything,

I only want to lie here
Forever and a day,
On this warm, talcum sand,
Beneath this looming dune,
Eating cheddar baked goldfish
With you.

Island Solitude

When wicked winter slams the panes,
Loads pitch pines with snow,
Counts its hourly gains
And into their snug warrens
Chases the rabbits,
And against their canine habits
Runs all domesticated dogs
And their masters into houses,
When the mind is gripped
By unruly winter's hand and
Blessedly ceases its antic pace,
Quieting the unsettled human race,
I like it that way.

When swirling snow drifts build for hours,
Blocking back roads, challenging the powers
That held sway just yesterday,
Wrapping cottages in a downy quilt,
Piling relentlessly against the doors,
Putting an end to daily chores,
When not a living soul comes to call,
No footfalls in the silent hall,
I like it that way,

When offshore winds howl and bay,
Buffet storm doors and play
Havoc with day and night,
Painting an offseason, tumultuous sight
In purest, inviolate white,
When no tracks of animal or man
Appear in the virginal snow,
Though I love you, you should know,
I like it that way.

A Keeper She Was

A keeper she was,
Youngest and loveliest
Ever at Cape Cod Light,
Whom I happened to meet
The night my ship went down
Off her coast, the outermost,

On the beach,
Thrown up by the sea,
I saw far above me
Beneath the beacon,
A phantom silhouetted
In the watch room light
That dreadful night,

She watched me struggle
For purchase
Beneath the battered bluff,
Her two strong arms pulled me
To safety atop the promontory,
I looked into the face of an angel
Mouthing words I could not hear
For the bellowing of the winds,

A lighthouse is a boon to pilots,
A beacon of safety, an aid to navigation
Warning of hidden shoals and reefs,
But not to dangers to the human heart,

All these years later, unseen by you
Distracted by the view,
We tend her lantern room together
In mild and stormy weather,
High atop the Pharos of Truro,
My lovely lighthouse keeper and I,
Beneath a blue and boundless sky.

Those Summer Days

You used to sing those summer days,
As we walked along,
Like a bird those summer days
You sang a lilting song,
You used to laugh those summer days,
Splash at water's edge,
Like a child those summer days
Who'd made a carefree pledge,
You took my hand those summer days
As we combed this beach,
Newly minted lovers,
Long love within our reach,
You used to skip those summer days,
Buoyant, happy, free,
Like a girl those summer days
When you were here with me,
These summer days when breezes blow
They haunt me with your song,
Your image locked in memory now,
To another you belong.

Cloistered

In the lee of an imposing dune,
In a cozy bunk below decks,
In an alcove at the
Brewster Ladies Library,
Beneath a beach umbrella,
At a lookout on a nature trail,
In a lighthouse keeper's room,
In a dune shack in a driving rain,
On an island,
Asleep in Davey Jones' Locker,
Piloting in a wheelhouse,
Parked in a beach lot at sunrise,
On the deck with the dog,
On a widow's walk under the stars,
Reclining in a bay window,
Last stool at the end of a bar,
Well inside a beach book,
Writing in a gabled dormer,
On a hideaway hammock,
Asleep in a bed tent,
In a lover's memory bank,
Sailing a single-hander,
Alone at a donut shop counter,
In an outdoor shower stall,
Moored in a secluded cove,
Sunning on a sand bar,
In the lee of your sheltering arms.

How Much Do You Love Me

How much do you love me, darling John?
How much do you love me today?

I love you more than a rosy dawn
Arising with bright display,

How much do you care for me, dearest John?
How much do you care today?

I care for you more than a pirate pines
For his gold well hidden away,

Is there nothing that you love, dear John,
Love far more than me?

One thing only, my darling dear,
A refreshing swim in the sea,

At that she turned and lovingly said,
It's quite the same for me.

I Took My Love To A Quiet Cove

I took my love to a quiet cove
Hidden from prying eyes,
She frolicked there in the blue-green sea
Beneath protective skies,
I watched her close, scanned our bay,
All the dunes around,
Found no intruders lurking there,
Heard nary a human sound,
My eyes were all her armor,
My vision her first defense,
My survey found no spying eyes,
No threats of consequence,
Yet as I looked more closely
At sky and sand and sea,
I realized Mother Nature's eyes
Were looking back at me,
Her ogling sun, pale-eyed moon,
Glass eye of fish and whale,
Were watching us with some intent
Behind a hidden veil,
I asked myself why all those eyes,
Those orbs both high and low?
Must nature long to see herself,
Her beauty 'gin to know?
Or could it be that just like me
She felt it was her duty,
To stare with such admiring eyes
Upon my lover's beauty?

Lines Written At The Jared Coffin House
Nantucket Island

A passionate shepherd I am not,
I've given sheep but little thought,
Nor is my love a phantom of delight,
From time to time she loves to fight,
Nor does she walk in beauty like the night
That only dreams to shine as bright as she,
Nor is she a Nicean bark of yore
Who only knows what perfumed seas are for,
Nor a temperate summers day
Who only breathes in lines that say
I loved you once, long, long ago,
Nor some bright, steadfast star is she,
I love her volatility,
Nor like Lucasta will she defer to war,
Inconstant loves bloody bore,
Nor will you find us meeting at night,
I would not have her out of sight,
Nor would she answer to "you come too,"
No afterthought for her would do,
Nor would I sum my love
Or love her better after death,
When I may taste her warm, sweet breath,
Neither is she a red, red rose
Or some coy mistress, yet I suppose
Some fancy only love's ideal,
I thank the gods my love's for real.

At The Marshside Bar

Every single thing I view
Suggests a fine compare with you,
Has no name in and of itself
Like odds and ends along this shelf,
All pointing back to who you are
In aspect, trait and quality, and
What, my love, you mean to me,

Vermouth reminds me of your youth,
Gin, that you occasion sin,
Whisky, need I mention frisky?
Red wine, so like my heart
Incarnadine,
What rhymes with lime
But sublime?
What's in a name? not Champagne,
Only yours,
Margarita, that my girl is sweeter,
Manhattan, that your skin is satin,
Single Malt, your rare gestalt,
Craft beers and ale,
Your sonneteer could tell a tale,

So it goes along the rail, without fail,
As each, in turn, suggests to me
Traits that only lovers see,
Who, like me, can never tame
The urge to everything rename,
Even at the Marshside bar

My thoughts are always where you are,
As every single thing I view
Suggests a fine compare with you.

Love Is Like A Sudden Rip

Love is like a sudden rip
That holds you in its potent grip,
Whene're you take a seaside dip
And inadvertent slip
Within its foamy clutches,
You feel its tugging current,
Resolve to swim to shore,
Yet swimming's no deterrent
Against this metaphor,
You struggle, soon exhaust yourself,
It pulls you out to sea,
Beyond the continental shelf
Where love wants you to be,
In deeper waters,
It needn't be that way, my friend,
You might have yielded soon,
Surrendered to love's potent pull
Been to its rips immune,
Swim to the side, swim to the side,
If you would save your hide,
To help your heart regain the land
Swim parallel to the sand.

At First Sight

What a foolish thing, love at first sight,
And it's only a boat, a handsome, little sailboat
Reflecting her sleek, classic image in the water,
Moored by herself within a broad, green, grassy
Marsh, bobbing gently on the placid water
As the breezes catch her half furled, single sail,
And what a sail it is, barn-red deepened with blue,
The best red, less ostentatious, less aggressive,
A deeply philosophical red, metaphysical even,
And here you are with me
Within this coastal Eden,

I covet you pretty, little sailboat,
I would like to stealthily loosen your mooring,
Board you, let you have your way with me,
And me with you, caress your polished woods,
Feel you move noiselessly under me
Across the shallow inlets,
Slip away with you farther up into the reedy marsh,
Then out to sea, each surrendering
To our joint desire for freedom,

I am captured by your image,
Your eagerness to sail,
Your simple, finely crafted lines,
I suspect someone placed you here
Just to catch my eye,

How content and proud you are to be so small,
So simple, yet possessed of everything
A sailor needs,
Or a freedom loving co-conspirator
Plotting his escape.

Cisco Beach

Keep your hearts well tethered,
This beach is a perilous place,
Yet its dangers may be weathered
With aplomb and practiced grace,

Gird your loins against the scene,
Keep your love in mind,
Remember where your heart has been
And what you'll never find
Again,

Don't look around or straight ahead,
Across or round about,
Appear to others good as dead
Or you may be found out,

Keep your wits about you,
Your heart confined within,
Don't cause a soul to doubt you
Or contemplate a sin,

Don't let yourself be seduced
By beauty, youth or charm,
Or your content may be reduced
Commensurate with the harm,

Like herring gulls stare out to sea,
Occasions of sin will pass,
No wiser warning can I give
To bonnie boy and lass.

Emerald Bright

Friend, capture for me
That time that has gone,
Those days when we lolled
By the sea,
Those days when her hair
Streaked with gold from the sun
And her eyes, emerald bright,
Captured me,

I can show you an image
All faded and cracked,
Tell you what I might recall,
But to capture the time
We spent by the sea
Would require a crystal ball,

Tell me then friend,
Did she love me those days?
Does she think of me
Fondly today?

Her eyes are as bright,
Gold gleams in her hair,
She waits
But a heartbeat away.

Forest Street Beach

Beautiful beaches are bittersweet,
Where waves, gulls and foredunes meet,
Where sapphire seas and pastel skies
Conspire at once to mesmerize,

Forest Street Beach is such a place
Where sea and surf daily trace
A scalloped edge along the sand
Curving in a winding band,
Littered with shells of snail and clam,
A glistening, shellfish scattergram,

You'll find no forest woodland here
Of oak or shrub or pitch pine near,
Just wide expanse of marsh and sea,
Terns and hawks your company,

Like a sailor seeking rest
I carefully chose her very best
Sheltering dune
From a sea grass berm, rough hewn,
Then settled in to block the breeze,
Take a vagrant traveler's ease,
Then gazed across at Monomoy
Till poignant thoughts diluted joy,

Beautiful beaches are bittersweet,
Cause the heart to miss a beat,
As all the beauty in one's view
Recalls what someone meant to you.

Bristol Beach

How long will I stay, you ask?
I will stay until my breathing
Synchronizes with the calming cadence
Of these waves,
My heartbeat aligns with the recession
And flood of the tides,
My soul finds a natural affinity
With the cormorant and the crab,
An easy kinship with the kestrel and the tern,
Until my mind adopts the patient pace
Of this natural world,
Until I tire of the bewitching beauty
Of your friendship, form and face,
How long will I stay?
For two eternities.

Two Years On

This coastline has no charm for me
Now lacking eyes to see what we two saw
In silence and in awe,
Overlaid on stream and rill,
Beach, orchard, wild-flowered hill,
Our shared, romantic, nature dream
That made her seem a heightened thing,
When then, as now, it's what lovers bring
That lends a magic to the view,
Dresses all in rosy hue,
Now every dell, dale and glen
Is burdened by remember when,
Every beach and kettle pond
Recalls our bond not their beauty,
Every seacoast hiking trail
Missing magic without fail,
Every dune, hilly flank,
Reminds it's you I have to thank,
I leave it all to those who see
What we two saw
In the efflorescence of spring,
The thrill a crashing wave can bring,
In the colorful canopies of fall,
Quiet water, oaken forests, all,
Something miraculous now is torn,
Two years on.

Summer Song

Why should I waste another day in vain
Crafting rhymes extolling all your beauties plain,
When haughty time in disregard of us
Will soon forget our love and all our fuss?
When vibrant verse beyond our stifled breath
Will not declaim for long beyond our death
The silken dreams I saw in you and you in me
Our loving eyes in briefest life did see?
When all our ardent, sunny days have fled
And all who knew your beauty then are dead?
When lifeless lips no longer can recite
And time has turned bright day to silent night?
No reason have I now to waste my days
In crafting lines in sundry ways to praise,
When here and now your loveliness is real,
And we may taunt old time and presently steal
A kiss, a look, a sigh, a fond embrace,
And from our flying, fleeting, fragile lives
Time's frowning visage swiftly chase.

One Summer Past

I coaxed a smile from a perfect face,
A tender smile of matchless grace,
That struck in me a chord so deep
That even now the years still keep
Its memory clear and front of mind,
I am certain I will not find
Another like it,

Her pale face averted, brightened then,
She blushed with a sudden, sanguinary glow,
I also know and clear recall
She would not turn to look at all,
From which I took some traction
In her lovely, brief reaction,

I will summon up her smile
Whenever life becomes a trial,
Which it became for me
The moment it faded from her face,
Leaving not a single trace
Of me, in her.

Beach Essentials

Decent forecast,
Folding chair,
Bathing suit,
Ready to wear,
Delicious drink,
No mind to think,
Wide angled view,
Near neighbors few,
A little lunch,
Something to munch,
A sandy nook,
A beachy book,
A towel and a parasol,
That's not all,
A lover's gaze,
All ablaze.

Twice Lucky Sun

Twice lucky sun that warms her skin
Then paints thereon a tan,
Too lucky sand she lies upon
As if it were a man,
Most fortunate sea that her surrounds
Caressing close her form,
Embracing all her beauty there
Whose liquid hands about her swarm,
Lucky gulls that call to her,
Then with stealthy pace
Circle round, make close approach,
To violate her space,
Full favored winds that muss her hair,
More unseen hands that find her fair,
While I am left to pine and stare
At one so fine sunbathing there,
Across this wide expanse of beach
So broad, so brown, so bare,
Whereon I labor long and lonely there
To build her a castle in the air.

Wild Caught

Some catch your eye and you embrace,
Some catch your eye, they tease,
Some catch your eye, you get a green light
To do whatever you please,

Some catch your eye, you covet,
Some catch your eye, they love it,
Some catch your eye, a mate you spy,
You quickly pretend you're above it,

Some catch your eye, you linger,
Some catch your eye, you stay,
Some catch your eye, you find new life
Day after glorious day.

Wood Neck Beach

Peak low tide, and the broad expanse
Of the waking beach
Had a lesson of wordless love to teach,
Few early morning walkers, no talkers,
Low, little waves still bashful and shy
Beneath the yawning, stretching sky,

He stopped every few feet,
Scanning the morning treasures
Scattered there beneath his feet,
Selected then a polished stone
From the heap night surf had thrown,
Then gently placed it in her hand
Where it fell against her band,
She received it in cupped hands
With silent gratitude,
True love's laconic attitude,
Where, in turn, he placed a cowrie,
A whelk, a cockle too,
Yet soon they moved beyond my view,

I climbed the dunes, left the beach,
Anxious for my love to reach,
Wondering if I loved that way,
Transcending words at break of day,
I found her waiting on our deck,
Her hands were cupped and I suspect,
Quite soon upon that very sand
White stones will fall against her band.

Cenotaph

I wish you wouldn't come today,
You put this beach to shame,
Its vaunted charms, its pageantry,
Now viewed by all as tame,
Your locomotion will eclipse
The movement of her waves,
Your lithesome body gods have made
Leads some to misbehave,
Your peachy cream complexion
Steals colors from her sky,
Your shapeliness and curves unnerve
Each and every passerby,
Your shyness and your charming laugh
Turn eyes away from her,
Her peerless panorama
Now just a fading blur,
I took you here one day last year,
It clearly was a gaffe,
Where once this beach
Stood proud and wide
Now stands a cenotaph.

You Are

More inviting than a beach at first light,
More protective than a hidden cove,
Gentler than an onshore breeze,
More dazzling than frosted sea glass,
More radiant than the midday sun,
More succulent than a lobster roll,
More faithful than the tidal ebb and flow,
More bracing than a late summer swim,
More mysterious than the sea at night,
More diverting than a shooting star,
Cozier than a blazing beach bonfire,
More graceful than a circle of mermaids,
More sheltering than a beach parasol,
Lovelier than a double rainbow,
More present than my sense of self,
Nearer my heart than the very blood
That courses through,
Are you.

Massacre At Howe's

Few are left to tell the tale,
The carnage of that day,
The awful human wreckage there,
The men who had to pay,
This is a story of seacoast lust,
Murder on the beach,
I'll tell you sir this story true
Since me you do beseech,

The sun was up and over hot,
Howe's was full of flesh,
Families here, couples there,
Each to each did mesh,
Umbrellas shielded some from heat,
Others crammed the sea,
If you were smart, survivors claim,
You wouldn't want to be
On Howe's that day,

Some say the tepid waters
Added to the strain,
Others claim congested sand
Led to what became a bloodbath,
Howe's, they say, was safe before,
Its gentle curve ideal,
Add to that its genteel waves,
Family friendly feel,
Yet those of us who sunbathe,
Yearly watch this place,
Took silent note of hidden things
That haunt the human race,

All women here are shapely,
Not one you might call plump,
Most of them maternal,
Each sunning on her rump,
The men are mostly docile,
Their muscled years behind,
Their manly powers waning now,
Though most of them not blind,
Unfortunately,

She suddenly appeared at noon,
I stood at water's edge,
My eyes fell out like Slinkies
Is what my friends allege,
She wore a black one-piece suit,
Her deadly weapon of choice,
She glided along the low tide mark
Suppressing every voice,

I saw them fall in bunches,
Some up against the dune,
Others dropped where they swam
In a bloody, briny swoon,
Her crime was planned well in advance,
Premeditation there,
This tall, svelte and striking girl
Had chosen what to wear,

When she had sashayed
Howe's full length
And every man was dead,
Few recalled just where she went
Or even what she said,

Today Howe's beach is full
Once more,
Teems with vibrant life,
Its powdery sands, pristine dunes,
Devoid of pain and strife,
One day she may again appear
As bathers swim and tan,
Friends be on your guard I say,
Wives protect your man,

I go sometimes to Howe's alone,
Reflect upon that day,
Weep for those who lost their lives
And the price they had to pay,
For looking.

South Cape Beach

Your only assignments
For today:
Pick a spot,
Not too breezy,
Not too hot,
Midway to the tidal line,
Where the sand
Is clear and fine,
There recline,
Turn over,
Open cooler,
Close cooler,
Turn over,
Wriggle your toes
Into the sand, and
Wriggle them again,
Then linger,
Tracing a love note
With your finger,
Take a dip,
Then another,
Kiss your wife,
Bow to life.

Some Windy Wicked Fearsome Stormy Day

Why waste a sunny day upon your love,
When such a vast array from heaven above
Presents her with a choice of many things
To distract her from the one she brings?
Observe her as she contemplates her choice,
Suppressing that soft and sweet romantic voice
That you, her lover, hoped to soon arouse
Where now those options vex her knitted brows,
Watch how long she tans beneath the sun
To keep your hugs and kisses on the run,
How carefully she lotions front and back
While thinking where she might obtain a snack,
See how she looks for love upon the page
Of some romantic novel now the rage,
Witness how her eyes engage the sea
Thinking how another dip might well be
Just the ticket, you're in a thicket,
If you would whisper, coo and hold her tight,
Avoid the glaring sun with all your might,
Come only when the sky is frightful dark,
When furious winds begin to light a spark,
When no distractions tempt her heart away,
Some windy, wicked, fearsome, stormy day.

Oh For A Life Nearby The Sea

Oh for a life nearby the sea,
A life of salt sea air and thee,
Oh for an endless string of days
To hold your hand, gaze and gaze
At all the wonders along the shore,
At all the beauty there and more,
At all the heaven in your eyes,
A paradise in other guise,
Oh for a life nearby the sea
Where every breath is pure and free,
Where souls may soar or simply be,
And only you for company.

Night Rendezvous

The curtain of night hung low on the beach
While a gray, ghostly mist kept you well within reach,
Sea pebbles that sang off in the dark
Suggested our visit was more than a lark,
You braved the chill air and the night rendezvous
While I held back the ardor my heart felt for you,
At the slightest suggestion you climbed up the ledge,
I followed behind grasping at sedge,
Giddy from height, fearful from night,
I held back my passion with all a boy's might
While the song of the beach made a wizard's delight,
You turned to me, closing your lovely green eyes,
Yet instead of a kiss I repaid you in sighs,
What you didn't know then that I knew all too well
Was a wild kiss of passion would have broken the spell,
And what might have happened if one of us fell?

Chapin Memorial Beach

Set back between wide marsh and sea,
Half hid among the sedge,
Her ruinous state beckoned to me,
Sad cottage set on ocean's edge,

Unnoticed by those speeding by,
Eyes riveted on the beach,
A rental shack, most humble, shy,
What might her modest aspects teach?

Yet to me, ambling by afoot,
Moved in equal parts by marsh and sea,
Her sandy decks, rusty chairs there put,
Suggested some romantic possibility,

I took her for the season of the sun,
Two lovelorn singles by the shore,
Waiting for the tide to flood and run,
Each battered heart desiring more,

I loved her long, she did the same,
No soul disturbed our peace,
We shared a summer romance there
And Chapin's wild caprice.

Women Will Not Stare

On a beach men will stare,
Even the sophisticated,
The bashful, the reticent,
Even the proper,
Who on all other occasions
Prudently heed the dictates
Of cultural appropriateness,
All men will look,
They'll gape and gawk,
Some may even try to talk,
They'll check you out,
Ogle, leer and my dear
Assertively stare,
It's part of their furniture,
They don't care,

Yet women will not stare,
On the beach or anywhere,
They'll not be caught at it,
Though they will check you out,
Subtly, swiftly, furtively,
Beyond the ability of
Man and machine to spot them,
They'll deploy a patented, undetectable,
Unseen, lightning quick, oblique glance

With an expressionless face
From a decent distance,
All without a perceptible
Turning of the head,
Except for those with minds like men,
Who'll stare as men do now and then.

All This Summer Long

If you knew, in your light heart
And purest mind,
Just how your very being affects me
On this day, on this fine beach,
How your charming walk, breeze-blown hair
Unhinge me, how your commentary,
Sweetly formed words, envelop me,
Impair my composure, cause me unease,
How your slender form transports me,
How your deep impression on all these others
Causes them instantly to part ways for us
Along the waters edge,
How your very presence unsettles
My known world, my customary composure,
Shatters like delicate crystal
The consensus reality I thought I knew,
Then, at that very moment,
Your tender, noble heart would skip,
Your precious breath would catch,
You could not take another step,
Nor could you speak or hold a thought,
So distracted out of mind would you be
That all onlookers would take swift pity on you,
As they have on me all this summer long,
If you knew, if you truly knew.

I Love The Cape & Islands

More than me?
What?
You heard me,
I didn't mean it that way,
What way?
The way you're now taking it,
How am I taking it?
The way I didn't mean it,
You don't say that to me,
You're not the Cape & Islands,
I'm being serious,
It's just an expression, and besides,
Everyone loves the Cape & Islands,
But I don't love the Cape & islands
More than I love you,
Maybe we should start over?
More than me?

Scargo Lake

She comes at night
From Osprey Lane,
Her image white and clear,
Her ghostly steps
Soundless, swift,
She harbors one great fear,

That she may miss her
Long lost love
Who waits for her each night,
By the lake, beneath the moon,
Illumined by its light,

She hurries to the landing
Whose gently angled slope
Conveys her spirit happily
Within the envelope
Of night,

She steps upon the little dock,
He turns and takes her hand,
It's then the moon conveys
Its light upon true love's command,

It ripples down across the lake,
Sparkling as it falls,
Heeding as it nightly does
Departed lover's calls,

They sit, look on in silence,
The lake imposes calm,
He pulls her close
To cut the chill,
Embracing arm in arm,

In time the summoned moonlight
Withdraws its golden glow,
Though you may spy them secretly,
You'll never see them go,

She comes each night
From Osprey Lane,
Her image young and sweet,
Her spectral steps so urgent,
Lost lover soon to meet.

Postcard

Come back
To the Vineyard,
Missing its magic,
Sulks in the sun,
Waves listless,
Gulls cranky,
Water tepid,
Mood all wrong,
Your beach chair's
Here on the deck
With your
Black Dog mug,
Something awful
Has happened
To the view.

Sea Nymph

She dragged me slain, weary and witless
Down immense volcanic slopes
Into her twilight, undersea haven,
Mortally maimed my certainties,
Quickly frayed the wedded clasp,
Added me effortlessly to her carnal trophies,
Transfixed my mind with her slutty grin,
Roused my very devil from his dank cell,
Yoked now to him, we swiftly fell,
Deeper beneath the waves,
She fractured the finest antique creeds,
Made base all decent deeds,
And with her slender form and seductive smile
Gleefully perched on the very rim of my debased
Heart, commanding all fair others to depart,
She roused the dormant blood, strangled
All the good I had pretended to,
Made merry my basest desires,
Made sport of my blushing countenance,
Girdled my confused spirit
With her brazen, subterranean wickedness,
Made me mindless and unwise
And with her piercing coral eyes
Quenched all desire for decency,
Placed a tarnished halo on my confused head,
Sang sea shanty's to my debasement,
Until the restoring rays of the rising sun
Released me from her sordid sorcery,
And I surfaced into the purifying light of day
Gasping frantically for a cleansing breath.

Memory Book

On this beach I witness
A slide show of memories,
Peruse an album of acquaintances,
Welcome a portfolio of persons,
Some living, some not,
Some missed, some better forgot,
I hear voices too, voices I once heard,
Distinctive ones, as vital as if their possessors
Were here beside me here on the sand,
Some I would give my all
To hear again in life,

This beach is a gathering place for ghosts,
Even this sun-dappled, boisterous beach,
Unbidden ghosts, delightful specters,
Amusing apparitions and some true haunts,
They arise in the mind spontaneously
Without encouragement,
And some, some very few,
Appear, then settle once more
Into the deepest, blood-red recesses
Of the chambered heart,
Where unsuccessfully they try to hide,
Where poignancy and searing loss reside.

To Mother Nature

When they extol your virtues
Don't take it so to heart,
They only mean to honor love
That stayed or did depart,
Your rolling waves of navy blue,
Your undulating seas,
Your fragrant flowers, wild and tame,
Are only used to please
A love, or to bemoan love's loss,
It's not to you such praise they toss,
Your amber colored sea grass,
Wind-whipped, coniferous trees
Are just a useful backdrop
To those who seek to please another,
Your awesome nights, glowing moon,
Setting sun, sandy dune,
Are simply props an ardent lover drops
His feelings on, I could go on,
This is not meant to wound you
Or take away your gifts,
You have a handsome face my dear
In need of no face lifts,
You'll always be in service
To those whose hearts are full,
With love that's found,
Love that's lost,

Emotions that will pull,
You'll always be employed my dear,
Yet beauty by itself,
Without infusion of the heart
Will sit upon the shelf.

Missing You

Missing you, who came every August,
I saved your prime tanning spot
Near to mine, up against the dune slat fencing,
Close by the "End of Public Beach" sign,
Just below the American flag,
Carefully, expectantly, marked your spot
With mother of pearl shells and driftwood
I gathered again this morning,

A stranger took your spot this year
Though I tried valiantly to save it,
Did you move away? stop renting nearby?
Get married? get sick?

I don't think you'll ever return,
Our summer pleasantries
Meant more than I knew,
I wonder what they meant
To you?

You'll never know
What you took from me,
From my dreams,
From this once too splendid beach.

The Only Fish In The Sea

At first she tried to trim my sails,
But I ran a tight ship
Old salt that I was, then
She thought me a cold fish,
I thought her broad in the beam,
Likely to rock the boat,
A loose cannon on my deck
Who would leave me
Grounded hard and fast
And swiftly take the wind
Out of my sails, so I clammed up,
Gave her a wide berth,
Fought to regain my sea legs,
Tried to fend her off,
And since I knew the ropes,
Nailed my colors to the mast
Intending to cut and run,
Ship out in high seas,
And sail close to the wind,
Yet soon I found myself
Swimming against the tide

All at sea,
She took some shots
Across my bow,
So I battened down
My hatches, and
After getting underway
Staggered about my lonely deck,
Fore and aft,
Three sheets to the wind,
Intent on smooth sailing
And a fine kettle of fish
For one,
I tried to keep an even keel,
Prayed for following seas
And fair winds, and
When becalmed I whistled
For the wind,
But often found myself
Adrift between the devil
And the deep blue sea,
Yet as the days wore on
Soon realized that for me,
My bonny lass was, in truth,
The only fish in the sea.

Bill's Blue Heart

So much depends
Upon,

A blue
Heart,

Glazed with
Longing,

Beside the white
Breakers.

And Yet I Do Remember

How odd, how foolish at my age
That I should call to mind
A young woman I once saw on this beach,
And strange, still hope to find,
Whose image one day seared itself
Somehow so deep in me
That though I am still happily wed
And raised a family,
My mind will summon up her face,
Her form, her gait, her smile,
As though some deeper part of me
Her youthful image did beguile,
It seems as though my heart and soul
Imprinted her within,
Though my life another way
With passion did begin,
Why now, when I have made my choice,
When my old heart is set,
Do mind and memory give a voice
To one I never met?
I have forgotten many things
Now that my life's September,
We never shared a single word
And yet I do remember.

The Gods Of Love

The darkening sky grimaced,
Puffed its formidable, inky cheeks,
Blew the startled, little sailboats
Into the nearest haven and
With fiery, narrowed eyes flashing,
Loomed like a peevish giant
Over the once placid beach,
Threw all bathers into a frenzy
As mothers claimed their children,
Fathers secured belongings,
And my love and I retreated
To a weather-beaten dune shack
To wait out, in sweet seclusion,
The slashing rains and moaning winds,
Compressed fury of a passing gale,
Where safe within, the gods of love
Did each of us regale.

I See Us There Again

I see us there again,
Undiscoverable from the land,
Invisible from the companionable sea,
Alone together, sipping Arabica
In two rickety, wicker chairs,
Wraparound, wooden deck dusted with sand,
Planked stairway loaded with it,
Upturned, peeling, red rowboat lying nearby
Against a matted field of beach grass,
Spartan lunch of black beans, brown bread,
And split pea soup on a reluctant camping stove,
All those soft words, your gentle laughter,
Our wild, untended garden of Beach Plum, Bayberry,
Dusty Miller, Sea Rocket, and Seaside Goldenrod,
One discreet gull atop the corner rail,
And we two intertwined the long, starlit night
Beneath an ancient, tattered quilt,
Letting the distracted world pass by,
I see us there again
In the mind's pained and longing eye.

As She Takes In The View

If you have found true love at last
Be careful on the beach,
The wise to me these thoughts have passed,
They have so much to teach:
Don't let her pale, unsullied soles
Make contact with hot sand,
Or let the scorching flames of sun
Upon her pale cheeks land,
Or suffer her to swim awhile
Where seaweed floats too near,
Or let her step on to a spot
Where crabs engender fear,
Or set her neath the piercing cries
Of petrel, gull or tern,
Or let her swim where waves are rough,
Where winds wild waters churn,
Shield her from the boisterous crowds
Who clump and cluster so,
Whose tone is strident, shrill and loud,
One last thing to know,
Don't take her to the beach at all,
Might lose her if you do,
For she may spy a newer love
As she takes in the view.

Bathing Beauty

She agitates the atmosphere,
Does something to the air,
Unsettles all the molecules
Just playing with her hair,

She flusters Mother Nature,
Disturbs her daily rounds,
Upsets the proper course of things
Her beauty so confounds,

She bothers other women
Who soon unsheathe their knives,
Her charm and loveliness so real,
She never sir contrives,

She stirs the blood and ruffles
What's tame and good and true,
Excites the animal in man
Whenever she's in view,

She bothers and she troubles,
Discomposes and distracts,
Suggests to all onlookers
Precisely what each lacks,

She agitates the atmosphere,
Old men begin to cry,
The charmless lift their eyes to god
Whene'er she happens by.

Remembrance

The hardest thing to do on a beach
Is call to mind a treasured love
Now far beyond your reach,
An even harder thing
Is to muster up the will to bring
This noble thought to bear,
With equanimity and grace
Upon the searing loss remembered there:
I will not mourn what I have lost
Or sacrifice this day,
I'm grateful for the time we shared
Though she has gone away.

Treasure Island

The beachcomber scanned his bar of sand,
A trove of gleaming gems in his hand,
He walked in a circle inspecting each stone,
True treasures within the tidal zone,
He gave each one a careful look,
Those that passed he eagerly took,
Those that failed he tossed away
With nothing to say that balmy day,

Above all he prized the heart-shaped stone
Some mischievous Cupid there had thrown,
Scattered among the varied shells
Thrown up by the tide and swirling swells,
Soon the tides reclaimed his isle,
And with a pleased and amorous smile
He handed his precious gems to her,
And not for a moment did she demur,
The heart-shaped stone did she confer,
On him.

Last Best Beach Day

The last, best beach day of the dying year
We each made a late day pact to honor,
And though haunted by workaday fear,
Boldly turned the insubordinate corner,
Two guilty hearts racing,
We laughed our way to the sunny shore,
None the wiser, for we had covered our trail,
And what is more
Each would have an escapist tale
To tell of hand holding at golden time,
When shadows are long, light sublime,
Of cool sea spray, of a late day getaway
To powdery sands,
Of a long, curvaceous, dune-backed beach,
As intoxicating, alluring, exquisite
As she.

Beach Bum

The bottom's often slighted
In prim, polite discourse,
Though it has oft delighted,
Been the splendid source
Of beauty and remorse,
Eyes and lips, even hips
Attract amorous attentions,
While the stalwart derriere
Merits fewer mentions,
The legs, the hair and the smile
Are thought to everyone beguile,
While the fleshy chap we sit upon
Quite appears forlorn,
Everybody has one,
Some it seems have more,
A perfectly shaped, bumptious bum
Is something to adore,
We catch a glimpse here and there
Sometimes upon a beach,
A finely chiseled derriere
Just beyond our reach,
It gets a final, critical glance
From women when they dress,
Yet seldom works its way within
Their discourse I confess,
It always lags a bit behind

Yet never seems to mind,
And everybody looks you know
Despite their inattentive show,
It's time the bottom had its day,
Say did you see her walk away?

The Names Of Stars

The staring, yellow moon sits
Full and low upon the silent bay,
Coastal lights blink on far off in Wellfleet,
A lone cormorant stands sentinel
On the shadowy breakwater,
A buoy bell sounds, then another,
The dying, driftwood fire crackles,
Throws off little flares that snap and pop,
As a wayward, onshore breeze musses
Your light-reflecting hair,
You shiver, I give you my windbreaker,
You smile and weakly protest,
We talk low of inconsequential things,
Lean back against the still warm sand,
I pretend to know the names of stars,
You pretend to believe me,
We slowly sip the sweet night air,
Our silence containing the same wishes
Each separately sends over the peaceful bay,
I take chaste liberties, you snuggle in,
The mischievous moon winks, then slow sinks
Into the open arms of the broad bay,
I give you three white stones
Polished to perfection by night waves,
You clasp them tightly and whisper,
"But I have nothing for you,"
Not true.

Wedding By The Sea

I've heard them say,
"I hear you'll give your child away,"
You have too,
Loud and clear in public view,
Yet who would say such a thing
Having only spied a ring?

You give away a book or chair,
Something you no longer care
To see or share,
You give away things
From which no deep emotion springs,
These you give, no strings attached,
Brief goodbye, door firmly latched,

You don't give away a child,
A wedded daughter's not exiled,
She's loaned and shared,
She for whom her father cared,
Though less robust, far less spry,
Her father keeps a whale's keen eye,
Watches her go and asks:
"Who will care for her as I?"
"Who?", a father wants to know
As he sees his daughter go?

Asked and answered
Here, today,
In this sacred, seaside place,
Before all of you.

Sail Away

If I should build a wooden boat,
Hoist a simple sail,
Would you sail away with me?
On you might I prevail?

If I should promise temperate winds,
Only following seas,
Would you come with me my love,
To feel the ocean breeze?

If I should plan for gentle swells,
Playful dolphin guides,
Briny, breaching, baleen whales,
Other joys besides,
Would you come?

If I should hang a lantern dear
From both the stern and bow,
Would you cast away all fear
And tell me here and now
You would?

If I should weigh the anchor,
Set course for magic isles,
By sparkling starlight reckon,
Would such a plan beguile?

If I should chart a lifelong course
From port to coastal port,
Along sequestered sandy strands,
What might your heart report?

If I arrange for shooting stars,
To light our way at night,
Flying fish to tag along,
Would such a wondrous sight
Convince?

If I conspire with sea and sky
To temper their extremes,
Would such inducement seem a lie,
The very stuff of dreams?

If I should promise all of these
And cooling, salt sea spray,
Would you share a berth with me
From the Cape to Bantry Bay?

Enough my love, I cannot fib,
We'll both put out to sea,
I like the cut of your jib my love,
I'll sail away with thee.

Fair Winds

View From Scargo Hill Tower

Freedom's friends are few,
Though she tries to breathe anew
In each new time, each new place,
She soon appears to lose her race
As autocrats her eyes poke out,
While the piously sermonizing doubt
She can or should live on her own,
Whether ripped unripe from out the womb
Or brutalized babe in early bloom
Few, for long, for her make room,
Power though like lots of dough
Has many friends, and suggests to most
Their ends may soon be realized,
Like her cousin control is highly prized,
Some soon declare what their intentions are,
Despot, tyrant, warlord, Caesar, czar,
While others bearing mild intent
Conceal their autocratic bent,
Like our moralizing values men
Who insist all live like them,
Self-righteous, coercive, hemorrhaging hearts
Take little note when soon departs
Freedom, liberty and choice,
Will no one give this child her voice?
Face it friend and foe alike,
Most of us would love to strike
A blow against this pure born child
We hardly know, for within the soul
Of each of us lives a demon blunderbuss,

Which yearns to righteously release
Our core values and beliefs on others,
Who if left in freedom's peace
Might well have been our brothers
And sisters.

Toreador Of The Shore

He takes an eager sprinter's start,
Launching himself upon the waves
With abandon, no thought but joy,
Airborne, as two outstretched arms
Do deploy high above the foamy spray,
Merging in a graceful dive today, then
Plunges neath the mountainous waves
Deeper into the chilly plumes,
Neptune's viscous rooms,
Then rises, sudden like Triton,
Bursting from the depths,
Bracing himself for the next
And the next and the next,
Watching each towering tumbler rise,
Then with a practiced mariner's eyes
Diving below each breaking crest
As each wave in turn he did contest,
Make the sea contend with you,
Toreador of the shore,
All of us are watching,
Be an artist, show us more.

Pride Of Place

To settle the matter amongst the three,
The majestic sky, soft sand and sea,
Resolved to make their case to me,

Sky demanded pride of place
Due to height and boundless space,
So too for all its varied moods
When sun shines clear or gray sky broods,

The sea claimed it could match the sky
For size, for blues that catch the eyes,
Best the sky with sound and feel
And all the creatures waves conceal,

The sand rebutted all they said,
Noting that all pathways led
To her, where every bather made a home
From which to sun, then beachcomb,

All day long they did contest
But could not settle on the best,
Yet if each could see with human eye
They'd soon declare a three-way tie.

Here And Now

How many others, like me,
Have wished to preserve this sun, this sea,
For another day, another time?
To borrow against some future sorrow,
Like foul midwinter or the mournful rain of fall,
When darker thoughts invade the mind,
Give the lie to the joy we've left behind?
How many others, like me, have sought to capture
The inexpressible rapture of a single beach day,
To spread it round the whole year long
Like a well-remembered summer song,
Whose lyrics would sound still loud and clear
Though woeful winter then be drear?
How many have tried and failed, as have I,
To take firm hold of sand and sky,
Only to watch each fly on by?
Since my attempts have come to naught,
I will recall what I've forgot and
All too often disavow,
We're only granted here and now.

Snapshots

Haley Hopkins lost her top,
Billy Brown his bottom,
Nether one will leave the sea
Though it's nearly autumn,

Haley Hopkins found her top,
Billy Brown his bottom,
They were not missed,
They hugged and kissed,
Soon everyone forgot 'em.

***

Baby had a diaper on
Before he took a swim,
Baby lost his nappy
Just after wading in,

Baby's bum is fat and round,
His legs are plump and short,
His mother chases after him,
Which is their favorite sport.

***

Baby's in the water,
Parents on the beach,
Lifeguard looks the other way,
Baby's out of reach,

Doggy's in the water,
Baby's on his back,
Doggy saves poor baby,
Baby's name is Jack.

Tom Nevers Night

Drunk with the silent, salubrious
Night, no longer fit for day,
Imbibing the moon's
Soft, shimmering light,
No longer can I say
What it was I saw before,
Beneath the sun, out of door,
Glaring lights, too active men,
Noxious noise, abandoned pen,
Frantic pace, loud reports,
Arena for contentious sorts,
Even flowers flaunt their wares,
Hubristic nature's garish flair,
Paramour now of the neighborly night,
Calmed by her mild and muted light,
Wanderer in her silent wards,
Attuned to all her subtle chords,
Inebriate soul out walking,
Emancipated from tedious talking,
I must renounce her counterfeit,
Proud, ambitious day, and
Send her boisterous acolytes
On their unconscious way.

Late Winter Visit

Bare were the flats below the cliff,
Dank her closed off rooms,
Pungent the sea beneath her there,
Dormant her springtime blooms,
Cozy the cottage wherein I wrote,
Perched high above the sea,
Where musty smells, off season scents,
Brought something to life in me,

O'er spread with sand her weathered decks,
Gloomy the gray quilt sky,
Empty the beach below my shack,
Designed to gratify,
Biting the nip of late winter wind,
Forbidding the deep, blue sea,
Yet oh what a glorious week I spent
Communing with only me.

Dionis Beach

Dionis delivers a rich array
At break of day,
When her morning glories
First strike the unprepared eye,
Yet again at night
When she paints another gorgeous sight,
The moment when you first let go,
When your psyche tells you so,
When first you greet her rising sun
That puts disquiet on the run,
When first you take in her expanse
That gives your soul a fighting chance,
The moment that your eager arms
Explore her water's ample charms,
The moment that you take a hand
To stroll along her soothing sand,
Surrendering to her rich array,
Hypnotic night, gilded day.

Whitman In The Surf

I hurl myself upon you waves,
Greeting each of you
With fellow feeling,
I let my pale, unapparelled,
Unblemished body move easily
Through your lusty, rising rollers,
Scattering the playful, skittish
Creatures beneath,
I jump, flop and turn, breaching
The surface again and again,
Like the baleen suborder of
Ecstatic lesser bottlenose,
Out of my seeking soul leaps
A satisfying communion
With your viscosity,
Out of my open mind
Run watery thoughts,
Out of my heart flow briny tears
Of wondrous, welcome delight,
Come wily wavelets, you know I
Am near, approachable, nude,
Ripe and radiant like you,
Limitless, untouchable,
Reverberating with life,
I crave your liquid joys,
Translate your rapture,
Feel you to your depths, my hoary
Hide of weathered skin
Merging with you, I see you too,
My warm, bold friend,

The lordly sky god,
Surround me wistful waves,
Touch my open soul,
Linger around this body
That is perfect, untainted,
Breathes vigorously like the sea
Beasts, through every
Gill and pore,
Witness me jump and spin, loll
About your liquefied precincts,
Witness my life force
Merge with yours,
O laughing gulls, fleecy clouds,
Dynamic dunes take note,
O fishers and sailors,
And scavengers,
Witness me here and now
As you and I proud sea,
Commune in sensate wonder,
As you and I vast ocean
Perceive boundless horizons,
As you and I together
Heal what needs healing,
Proudly promulgate
What needs proclaiming,
I caress myself without shame
As do these wanton waves,
I lick sweet sea salt from my lips,
Make easy love to your depths,

I ponder how to bottle this joy
For all my brothers,
For I am in the life,
Am the life and may not be
Enjoined, impeded or chastised
By man, god
Or your exalted institutions,
Toyed with or trampled by fate
Or mind
Or self appointed authorities,
I revel, prance, snort, gambol,
Make silly, raucous play,
Catch the potent present with long
Powerful casts of my reel,
My democratic, pluralistic,
Weightless soul rising
Like a child's box kite
Into the ether, while gratefully
I hum a familiar, patriotic hymn
To your open canopy of sky, and
Not a one can temper
My happiness,
Not a one can break off
My bare bathing,
Not a one can impede
My freedom of movement,
O unclothed loins,
O liberated flesh,
O much maligned,

Pelagic predators,
My merry, maritime brothers,
O sultry, summer season
Of lubricious joy,
A child said, "what is a wave?"

Eliot On A Sand Bar

La famille en vacances.
Sick transit gloria mundi.
Non disturbare per favore.
Savez-vous planter les choux?

I make my visit like these pale,
Despondent others,
Like fashionable Mr. Tendentious
I take tepid, green tea
With a generous dollop of ennui,
Smelling sadly of lupine to me,
There's still time,
To be singed, to be scorched,
Time for my life to be torched
Here with these dead and desiccated
Upturned crabs,
Entrails visible from the pecking
Of the wretched, vacuous gulls,
Dragged by the horrid, wimpy wavelets,
To the water and back,
Past time to get my life off track,
Rue my first marriage,
All rhyme and joy disparage,
Is that a crack in time
I hear them say?
Has John of the Cross gone away?
Has spoliation come to stay?
Now that they're on their way,
What would Picasso say?

Where is Yves Montand today?
Let's be beleaguered
Like these sea-washed boulders,
Aching with heat, clutched
By baleful barnacles,
So not a space remains,
Then you know it rains,
And I put on a face
For the fawning ones,
Sense the aloof universe
Plotting my demise
And no one even tries,
I press myself against a raft,
Am I daft or can I craft
An obfuscating word or two
That might confuse
One of you? leaving me blue,
La-di-da, la-di-da,
I tear up, scowl at their pretense,
I mean to say I really do,
Shall I pull my onepiece suit way down?
Wear a modern, supercilious frown?
Or is my relief so very brief,
Drowning just off Gloucester there,
As the dainty devil
Mutters a muddled prayer?
What would poor Miro do?
Or the odd, curmudgeon Camus?
Is Modigliani through?
What did I hear them say?

Will Madame Crankshaft wish to play
Canasta, poker, later today?
Is sacerdotal priestly or merely beastly?
Why all these dried
And scabrous bits
From off my face? do I dare trace
A dispiriting symbol in the sand?
Or on a foreign strand?
Oh why this fetid smell?
Is the brackish, mangled marsh unwell?
Perhaps Maimonides will tell?
Why those seashells all broken there?
And all those tiny suits they wear?
Do I dare wear underwear?
I am by seaside sensuality quite undone,
Scanty, scanty, scanty,
I am the death of fun.

Sandy Neck

The sea spread out to greet the sky,
The sand, so white, so pure,
Euphoria written in her eye,
My love, so young, demure,
Our perfect spot lay near the surf,
Not too close, too far,
A sparkling bit of coastal turf
Upon this vast sandbar,
Our blanket fluttered in the wind,
We toasted with white wine,
I settled into paradise
With my valentine,
When a lone greenhead fly,
Reconnoitering the shore,
Gave us both the evil eye
Deciding to explore,
He buzzed and bit, we tipped the wine,
We swatted, stood and flailed,
Our backs, our arms, our suntanned legs
This menace now assailed,
Our sandwich fell upon the sand,
Walnut brownies did the same,
He's over here, he's over there,
He's awfully glad we came,
I hyperventilated,
Blood pressure climbed apace,
Our hopes and dreams of paradise

One insect did erase,
We fled the beach, our peace destroyed,
The greenhead moved along,
Harassing every couple there
Immersed in love's sweet song.

True Democracy

True democracy exists
Only on a public beach,
Thrives there, flexes its potent,
Constitutional muscles,
Easily models pluralism
For those who find
Political abstractions difficult,
Welcomes all, tolerates all
Without exception,
Displays colors, sizes, behaviors,
Modes of dress and undress,
More varied,
Unique and all encompassing
Than a dense, sophisticated
Urban center,
Throws us all together:
The trim, the ample,
The attractive, the well bred,
The charmless, the loud,
The asocial, the boorish,
The sophisticated, the vulgar,
The inhibited, the angry,
The kind, the selfless,
The sanctimonious,
The exhibitionist, the ascetic,
The cold-hearted, the civil,

The perpetrator, the victim,
The compassionate, the chatty,
The irresponsible, the catty,
The high-minded logician,
And the gustatory sensualist,

Only here on a public beach
Is found the living
Embodiment of the revered,
Iconic New England town
Meeting, the seaside manifestation
Of true human equality,
And our long admired, yet only
Partially realized capacity for
Transcendent, human tolerance,
And non-judgmental coexistence,

Every high summer,
As I take in this amazing,
Heartening, hopeful, inspiring, Utopian scene
In all of its noisy, multifaceted, Glorious wonder,
Deeply touched, full of sentiment, Shaken to my core,
Suffused with an idealistic dream
Of political, democratic and
Humanistic oneness,
I think to myself:
Maybe I'm not a democrat.

Man's Best Friend At Quidnet Beach

Ancient Plautus said it best,
Homo homini lupus est,
Man's been a wolf to his fellow man
Since our troubled world began,
Though the ravenous wolf begat the dog,
What an ironic epilogue
To find that man's best friend indeed
Fell straight from such a lupine breed,
While the seed that Eve begat
Should carry such a caveat,
Prescient Plautus said it best,
Nor was his warning said in jest,
Homo homini lupus est.

What Rhymes With Beach

What rhymes with beach?
What is synonymous,
Essentially eponymous?
What sounds the same
That you can name?

What strikes the ear as very near?
What hits the heart
As though a dart was thrown?

What suggests propinquity,
Nearness in place and time,
Not unlike a rhyme?
What conjures up
The self same thing?
Does a bell so clearly ring?

"Joy" for one and "beauty",
Clearly "fun", then there's "run"
And "dive"
And so the human soul may thrive,
There's also "tan," and "veg," and "sun,"

What rhymes with beach?
So many things beyond the reach
Of those who deal in rhyme.

Sudden Squall

Now the bilious breezes blow,
As wind-lashed whitecaps foam and crest,
While threatening clouds hang well below
In agitation quite distressed,
Now all vessels head for shelter
As seafarers plot safe course,
All about is helter-skelter,
Mother Nature's tour de force,

Now all whales, all fish, dive deeper,
As thunder, lightning, sound and crash,
No more the breaching, joyful leaper,
To frolic topside's far too rash,
And we bathers caught outside,
Exposed to nature's fit of pique,
Scan our shoreline far and wide,
Some safer haven there to seek.

Modern Malady

What malady is this
Accompanies me to this fine beach?
Spreads its towel near to mine and
Chatters on though my own tongue be mute?
Summons past to rouse regret,
Summons future to wake new fears and yet
I know it well, as if another skin I'm in,
My very own, mind-fashioned haunt,
Ever destructive of joy and leisure,
Eager still to poison pleasure,
My toxic companion, lingering louse,
Unwelcome guest in my very own house,
Producing anxiety and unease faster than
This beach can apply its fabled antidotes,
So, after moments of irresolution,
I retrace my path up through the escarpment,
And at the nearest post
Tie mind off with ligature and lock,
So at last I might take stock
Of the beauty here,
Stolen summer moments dear,
Yet as I swam, as I tanned, as I felt my soul
Soar with the breeze,
I still perceived a vague unease,
Mind waited for me atop the rise
With dark intent and demon eyes.

Who Gave This Wondrous Sea

What more could you want from Me
Who gave this sky, this wondrous sea?
Eyes and ears and flesh to be
What I might be through you?
Birdsong, married love,
Twinkling orbs above,
Children, parents, music, sleep,
Precious things that you might
Keep for a time,
Life enough to thrive,
Partnered rapture while alive,
Gentle death to end all pain,
Sleep inducing, nighttime rain,
Minds that might perceive the joy
Dispensed to every girl and boy?
So when I call you home one day,
Please no attitude, only gratitude,
What more could you want
From Me?

What Kind Of Creature

What kind of creature would you be
If you were not my child?
A lobster on the floor of the sea
Scavenging in the wild?
Perhaps a seal within a pod
With rounded face, unshaven,
Or maybe a soaring shorebird
Aloft in Vineyard Haven?
What kind of creature would you be
If you could make a wish?
One with gills and wonderful wings,
A fantastical, flying fish?
What kind of creature would you be
If I should turn and count to three?
A dolphin heading out to sea
Far, far away from me?

Dear Mother, I'd choose again
To be your child and
Pass on all those in the wild.

Nature's Radiant Face

Whose face does nature's radiant
Face conceal,
And fails in our short span
To scarce reveal?
Whose majesty lies cloaked
Behind a veil?
Whose grace and blessings
Billow every sail?
Blowing the souls of men
Through one quick life,
Charting our earthbound course
From joy to strife,
And back again?

What bashful Being will not
Look us in the eye,
Or satisfy our questing souls
To give us reason why?
Such questions haunt
The human mind
But not the human heart,
Which does not ask
For probative proof
In lieu of nature's art,
Extrapolates from beauty, bounty,
Babies, life and love,
To posit something deeper,
Something far above,
Leaving the pending legal case

For those
Whose minds require
Someone to depose,

Content am I reclining
On this sand
To live with mystery,
No further proof demand,
Than what my heart, my soul,
My senses here do feel,
Content to let her pretty face Paternity conceal.

Your Heaven In Disguise

What might you find in Heaven sir
You could not find right here?
Don't look god's gift horse in the mouth
With paradise so near,

I've known your charms,
Your sun, your surf,
I've tanned long days serene,
I've sailed, I've swum,
I've found true love,
All coastal joys did glean,
I've feasted with my eyes and ears,
Seen you tame the mind,
Yet I am restless, full of fears,
And must a Heaven find,

But what if what you seek is here,
Right before your eyes?
This water world, this beach, this day,
Your Heaven in disguise?

You needn't try to win me Shore
To such a tempting thought,
Like other men I crave yet more,
Like other men am caught
By the dream of eternal life.

Woman Of Comfort

I'm a woman of comfort, I stare at the sea,
A man of ambition lies here next to me,
Each in a chaise with a tonic Bombay
Reclining and whiling our soft lives away,

We gaze at the sun as it sinks in the west,
We pick at pink salmon, wild caught is the best,
We have what we aimed for, the good life of ease,
We lounge and we feed, we do what we please,

Our home is a showplace for you to admire,
We got what we aimed for, never aimed higher,
Our days are quite pleasant, warm 'neath the sun,
We've solved all our issues, except maybe one,

I'm a woman of comfort, no life of the mind,
I devour sweet cakes, am that way inclined,
I focus on lifestyle, gratify my desires,
Of comfort and ease my heart never tires,

I seldom reflect and mingle with those
Whose lifestyle and status align I suppose,
I cultivate pleasures for me and my spouse,
Lounge on plush sofas throughout our beach house,

One day by our pool with its view of the sea
My proud, portly husband slumped down next to me,
Taking note of my stare, then averting his head,
He wondered aloud if we're already dead.

All The Beauty Fair

I leaned against a driftwood log
Upon an empty beach,
A friend and I sat side by side
Each disinclined to preach,
I asked if all the things we saw,
All the beauty fair,
Suggested that behind our world
Lay some creation there,
He would not hear a word of it,
His brain had told him so,
Natural selection had caused
Our world to grow,
Yet, he said, if you have need
To find creation there,
It's nothing but more evidence
Of your precepts doctrinaire,
But, I said, can you be sure?
Can't you leave room for doubt?
Does not this coastline's majesty,
Profoundly, clearly shout
Prime Mover?
Pure myth, he said, there is no source,
No Architect behind,
I pray that you would soon like me
Take counsel from your mind,
You mean that meager, three pound sponge
Sits atop your head?
I'd rather take wise counsel friend
From heart and eye instead.

An Ocean View

I always require an ocean view
For traveling, dining, vacationing too,
Whatever it is I choose to do,
I need, I crave an ocean view,
I can't explain my odd obsession
Nor do I credit decompression,
I think instead it's just a form
And quite the norm of regression,
For those, like me, who seek our roots
Where soul and sea are in cahoots.

Beached

Scientists are quite perplexed,
Year on year increasingly vexed,
To find that Boston's famous
Firms are stranding
on the sandy Berms that line
The Cape & Islands,

They understand that client fees
Might cause some firms
To put to seas,
Yet can't discern the major cause
That might explain why
women of Laws, men too,
Would beach themselves
Within full view,
Why wouldn't open ocean do?

Was a partner in distress?
One who made a wicked mess?
In which event a firm's cohesion
Might constitute sufficient reason
For a mega-firm to strand
Beneath a dune
O'er topped with sand,

And do we even need
To mention
All the media attention
Such strandings would entail
For senior partners
Fine-toothed whale?

Or perhaps this was a way
For younger lawyers just to say,
Goodbye to those infirm and old
Who drain the firm
Of funds I'm told,
Or maybe they were
Trailing prey in search of
One more billing day?

Whether weather, food or Quakes,
it hard to say
Just what it takes
To beach a firm against a berm,
Who wouldn't feel an instant pity
For a firm from ones home city?
Nor do we suggest
The gallows for lawyers loitering
In the shallows,

So if you spot a stranded firm
In pinstriped suits against a berm,
Take the higher moral ground,
Especially on Nantucket Sound,
And treat all species, though
Rapacious, as you would
All those cetaceous.

Benefits Of A Beach Belly

Malleable, tractable,
Easily maneuvered to the right,
To the left or to block a view,
Suggests an amiable nature
Whether the paunch possessor
Is or is not,
Unthreatening, arouses no envy,
Laughs when you laugh,
Jiggles, sways and dances,
Encourages one to stay
In a fixed position
Assuming one wishes to so remain,
Cushions frontal blows,
Creates shore rapport
By mimicking the undulations
Of the heaving sea,
Occasions mirth if sufficient girth,
Provides the semblance of companionship
When there is none,
Accommodates a robust feast,
Provides a broader canvas for tanning,
Lowers male threat levels,
Always takes the point in travel
And in danger,
Provides the buoyancy of a life jacket
And ample stores in times of scarcity,
Is pregnant with meaning and
Contains nothing extraneous
For it's all subcutaneous.

Home Port

Who would exalt the sea eagle
Over the golden?
Honor the humpback
Over the horse?
Esteem the coast
Over the countryside?
Elevate the shore over the plains,
Or take special pains
To evaluate and compare?
Who on god's, great earth would dare?

Still many have noticed, as have I,
That every step away from the shore
Causes a minute but detectable
Contraction of the soul,
Tightening of the breath,
Compression of the heart,
Constriction of the feelings,
Narrowing of the view
And in all but a few,
A small but perceptible diminution
In one's capacity for undiluted joy,
All of which suggests that
Our largely liquid spirit
Invariably shrinks
The farther we roam
From our watery home.

When Chatham Town Is Fast Asleep

When Chatham town is fast asleep,
Its ocean discontent,
Its wintry winds contentious
And its low grey sky is rent
By the sweep of the Light,
Look for a tall, wan, young girl
Emerging from the deep,
Her restless soul, heavy heart,
The ocean cannot keep,
All in black she walks the beach
Searching for her kin,
Scanning its broad, sea-grass reach,
Moaning above the din,
Her clipper foundered
Two hundred years ago,
Not far from where she wanders now,
Little more we know,
If you stand above the beach,
Listen with all your heart,
You'll hear her muffled, mournful cries
To once again be a part
Of the family she lost,
Don't look her way, dare reply,
Speak or meet her eye,
If you do she'll stop and stare,
Her sorrow borne upon the air,
In the middle of the night

When Chatham Light
Sweeps the beach,
Look for a lovely, lonely wraith
The secret sea will send,
A sad, distraught, inconsolable girl
Whose heart will never mend.

Relaxing At Pocomo Beach

Overcast since we got here, great whites just offshore,
The Evil Empire's back, engine light's on,
Umbrella's airborne, everyone's on a cell phone,
Sand fleas in my suit, dear ticks got smaller,
Car keys under the sand, downwind from smokers,
Greenhead at ten o'clock, colon exam next week,
Get reviewed next week, aliens built the food pyramid,
An entire law firm beached itself, free speech on life support,
Tips secretly added to bills, my only jeans are dad jeans,
No representation without taxation, no food is good for you,
Moral high ground's congested, editorial pages metastasized,
I can't see over myself, We The Government,
Group rights, no due process in the Academy,
The Bard of Avon's a fraud, can't inflate the float,
She said we could still be friends,
No one can decipher hospital bills,
Sunblock in both eyes, the NSA monitors my thoughts,
Imperial Hubristic Presidency, political Supremes,
Spendthrift Legislature, debtor nation,
They forgot the mayo and the mustard,
This public beach is 5 by 8 feet, boom box at 8 o'clock,
The entire grid's at risk, the right's intolerant,
The left's irresponsible, Burundi just got nukes,
I'm a single heartbeat from eternity,
My sullen son grabbed the last beach chair,
Relatives just arrived at our rental.

Sea Fever

First Mate:
Captain, do you see this wondrous sea?
Same sea that I see?
So deeply moving, awe inspiring,
Teeming with myriad life forms?
Each a miracle of creation,
Each creature containing a kind of pelagic
Soul, fashioned from an all-knowing
Imagination, all worthy of preservation?
The soul stirring, variegated
Colors of the heavens here,
Cerulean, cyan, turquoise, sapphire?
Do you sense the gentle rocking of our vessel
As if by some celestial hand lovingly held?
Do you feel the wind-lashed spray
Upon your whiskered, sunburned cheeks?
The sweetly salted spume rising from off the
Sea to encourage us in our daily labors?
Hear you now the distant shoreline
Calling us back to port like a prima donna
Throwing her powerful contralto
To the farthest rows of this watery theatre?
Oh my billowing, awakening, ecstatic soul,
I cannot look about or rob one fish of life,
All the beauty here confounds me,
Cuts through me like a knife.

Captain:
You've caught sea fever matey,
Been at sea too long,
We'll get you back on firm, dry land
To sing the lubber's song.

Bright Burden Of A Sunny Day

Coercive, too conceited sun,
Who when the summer night
Has run, wakes us all with your
Bold, unsubtle blast,
Who made you the boss of me?
Who long ago decreed
That you should be
The driver of our midyear days?
Too glittering goad who, like a tyrant,
Dictates all must rise and shine,
Though some, like me, quite often pine
To trod another path,
If in doing so we might avoid
Your gilded, guilt-inducing wrath,
I wish for a slate and rainy day,
A respite from the beach,
Hiatus from the do, do, do,
What god might I beseech?
Today I'll lie inert abed,
Resist your sunlit charms,
Devote myself to books instead,
Rebuff your bright alarms.

Too Much Information

Nothing so offends
The tender sensibilities
Of New England bathers,
The natural serenity
Of a midsummer beach day,
The fragile sensitivities
Of the young at play,
The innocent expectations
Of the newly nubile
And the natural order
Of all things at waters edge,
Than an elderly man
Wearing a barely-there
Bikini bottom,
Who with false bravado
And feigned disinterest,
Parades alone along the seafront
Before imagined admirers,
Who, all mortified,
Avert their disbelieving eyes,
Cradle their whimpering young,
And, to a bather,
Mutter infernal imprecations
Against the peripatetic perpetrator.

The Heart Opens

The heart opens wide here on the Cape & Islands
Sometime between Thanksgiving and New Years Day,
Full, throbbing red, genuine, unconstrained,
From beneath the cold, bony New England chest,
Sweetly, innocently awakens from its year long dormancy,
Eager to spread good wishes,
"Love" even, a concept normally far too intimate
And emotionally powerful for the native ear,
Except of course this time of year,

A deep feeling of good will and geniality,
Abetted by cloying holiday music and affecting jingles,
Springs suddenly to life, struggles up
Through the early winter crust,
Peers amiably through frosted windowpanes,
Suppresses our prized, righteous reserve,
Rescues, redeems and celebrates our shared humanity
With a demonstrative, wintry luminescence,
Fog like floods our fields, forests,
Salt marshes and shorelines,
Unashamedly sending good wishes
To newcomers even, dear god forbid,
Then, just after New Years Day, is hid.

The Gull And The Crab

I waded cautiously into the surf when a blue crab warned me off,
In slow retreat three feet ahead, sharp pincers raised aloft,
I turned around, retraced my steps, he secreted himself in the sand,
I marveled at his defenses, a true predator in command,

When all of a sudden a herring gull snatched him
Clean right out of the sea,
Transported him in his yellow beak to a tidal pool near me,
Blue pincers that had warned me off flexed now to no avail,
They could not reach the gulls broad head, white belly, feathered tail,

The gull then dropped him onto the sand, dismembered him alive,
A violent, piecemeal, savage attack, no blue crab could survive,
His legs were ripped, an eye was pierced, wide carapace pecked away,
As a clever scavenger of the deep succumbed to a bird of prey,

I struggled to find a lesson there, some moral point of view,
How might I overlay good and bad on a pitiless pas de deux?
I did not want to acknowledge the lesson of what I'd seen,
That nature's rules are nature's rules, neither kind nor mean.

Sand On The Bed

Oh dear, oh dear, there's sand on the bed
Is what my meticulous mother said,
Oh dear, oh dear, there's sand on the floor,
Who forgot to shut this door?
Oh dear, oh dear, there's sand in the car,
I'll find you out, I know where you are,
Oh dear, oh dear, there's sand in these shoes
Is how my mother sang the blues,
Oh dear, oh dear, there's sand on this sheet
And with that I beat a retreat.

Unforgiving

Bathing suits are unforgiving,
They bunch, they rise, they cling,
They rarely flatter for that matter
And despite affirming chatter,
Seldom show to best advantage
All ones subject matter,

Forget your fatal flaw or three,
Your suit informs against thee,
That very thing you would conceal
Your suit's too anxious to reveal,
Your ample bum, concave chest,
Are all too soon by suits confessed,
Your uncut abs, spindly legs,
Your suit too quickly begs
To display and what is worse,
On the most sunshiny day,

Thank your lucky stars for clothes,
Human hotness seldom goes
To the beach, where flaws are bared,
Too soon displayed,
With another's eyes you'd be dismayed,
Bathing suits are unforgiving,
Each and every one,
Pay heed to doubts and all misgiving,
Unless you're twenty-one.

Reclamation

With his child near the sea
Fathers soon regress,
While mothers maintain dignity
Lost innocence the less,
A castle with elaborate walls
Dad's craft for hours on end,
With purest, unaffected joy
To such a task descend,
They'll drop into the shallows,
Mimic crab and whale,
Breach much like a dolphin,
Commence to bob and flail,
They'll play with shovels,
Pails and nets,
With flippers, floats and toys,
Collapse the span of years between,
Becoming little boys,
The man you thought
You knew so well
In office, home, or street,
Transmutes right there
Before your eyes
To someone really neat.

The Beach At Night

The beach at night is full of fright,
Not from things that tug and bite
Within the light of day,
But scary, scruffy, scabrous things
That chill the soul, lead some to pray
And other fearful folks to stay
Safely within doors,
Threatening, unspeakable things
The sun-drenched day deplores
And with its warming, daytime rays,
Sun all too soon restores,

Dark and dire, dreadful things,
With scales and jaws on silent wings,
Specters, ghosts that make the most
Of the cloak of night,
Alien things that shine a light,
Quick secrete you out of sight,
Distressing things that fill the head
With dread as they menacingly spread
Over the disquieted shoreline,

Things that seize
Upon a sudden, nightly breeze,
Appalling, shocking, daunting things
That in the day do vanish
And despite how much you pray

All invocations banish,
Don't walk the path you walked today
Or linger on the beach,
In dark of night with scarce a light
You are within their reach.

A More Receptive Heart

Along this shore I know far more
Than ever books can teach,
Than might be found in words or thoughts
Or proud, impassioned speech,
I also know and here possess
A more receptive heart
Than the one that beats on city streets,
They seem two poles apart,
But could I keep this wider heart
When I return to home,
I'd hear there sounding in my soul
Compassion's metronome.

Top Ten

The quest to rank a beach as great,
As perfect or as best,
Has for the ranking mind of late
Become a crucial test
Of whether moments spent thereon
Are worth your time and rest,
Rating now is all the rage
As bathers north and south engage
In estimating worth, yet
To me such foolish games
Should more occasion mirth,

A beach must have soft, silken sand,
Gently rolling waves,
A pleasing water temperature,
A crowd you find behaves,
A wider width, a gentle curve,
A soft and sandy bottom,
Yet few can boast of all those things,
Most just haven't got 'em,
For heaven's sake don't rank your beach,
Leave metrics to the mind,
The best is where your heart resides,
Fond memories there to find.

A Welcome Rain

We wake by the shore to a downpour,
A steady, showering, shushing
White noise of a most welcome rain shower,
A driving, drenching, muscular, heavy rain,
A proper, coastal cottage enveloping rain,
Born of a cloudburst, quickly maturing into
A continuous, unceasing, unbroken flood,
With none of the drizzle, sprinkle,
Intermittent teasing, drop by meager drop
Rain of most days,
Nor is it the feisty, boisterous, torrential rain
Of thunderclaps and bright bolts of lightning,
Whose energy promises much,
Yet too quickly spent, soon exhausts itself
In deference once more to the imposing sun,

We silently encourage you rain, cheer you on,
Wish for you to crowd out the light
And tedious warmth of this midsummer day,
To rout and occlude the smug sun,
To help us delay all doing,
All wholesome outdoor activity,
While we snuggle in and lovingly linger here
In our homey hideaway
Perfecting the elusive art of doing nothing,
We welcome your monsoonal music,
Your sodden, symphonic chords,

And securely sheltered herein
Will love, write and play undisturbed,
Witness how swiftly you slow our breathing,
Never was inclemency so damned delightful,
Come comforting rain, surround, inundate,
Precipitate.

Great Hollow Beach

How peopled is this sandy place,
How diverse in size, shape, age and race,
How stuffed with forms, with pitch of voice,
How such a strand might well rejoice
To witness all who've come to her,
To her soft sands and surf defer,
Fleshy babes who squat and tap
Against small waves that foam and lap,
Muscled lads who strut and play
Whose sinewy forms to all display,
Nubile girls who lie and tan,
Soon alter all attention span,
Mommies tending to their young
With modulating mother tongue,
Businessmen of formidable face
Who cannot yet their week erase,
Mum introverts who read and think
Engaged with page and pen and ink,
And the old, now slow of gait,
Whom sun and breeze invigorate,
A myriad of floaters, boaters, joggers,
Walkers, eaters, greeters, endless talkers,
The prim, the prude, the riotous rude,
All are here,
How peopled is this pretty place
With our compacted human race.

The Fates Who Spin Allot and Cut

Of all the souls upon this beach
Whose life would you take in trade?
If you could, if they would,
If yours were too in the shade?
Whose motley mix of joy and sorrow
Would you happily borrow?
If you could swap your life for theirs,
Wake in theirs tomorrow?

That little girl's whose kite just caught
A strong, uplifting breeze,
Whose life will end within the year
In tragedy overseas?
That handsome man's with lovely spouse
Who strolls this sandy mile,
Whose secret affair will cause despair,
Leave each in deep denial?
That portly man's who owns the home
Proud sits upon that rise,
Whose martial son will die next week,
His soul soon traumatize?
That ingénue's there next to you
Who's life seems free of strife,
Who in the coming wintertime
Will quietly take her life?

Envy not another's fate,
Their jumble of joy and woe,
Embrace the little life you got,
There's much you do not know,
The Fates who spin, allot and cut
Wove a life for you,
This time, this place, your special grace,
Today this lovely view.

Clambake

Anshuli, Tawana, Jack,
Vlad, Carmine, Ali and Wei-Lin,
Enjoyed a clambake on the beach,
Then they all dived in,
Guns fell silent,
Projections were withdrawn,
Tribal memory and grievance
Were transcended, thereby
Rescinding human history,
The Other became the One
Under the same old, jaunty sun,
Us and Them merged seamlessly,
And the United Nations,
Upon unanimous agreement
Of all nation states,
Happily revoked its charter,
A single, harmonious tribe was born
Upon the earth
And a single, auspicious narrative
Arose spontaneously
From the many.

Girl In Yellow

Dancing there at water's edge
A gay, young girl in yellow,
Twirling, spinning, turning,
Eyes closed, head held aloft
In the spindrift air,
A delightful, daring dervish now,
Splashing in the modest waves
Within a shower of salty spray,
Light footed on the spongy sand,

She raises her new arms
In exuberant joy,
Whirls, wheels and pirouettes,
Her mind now powerless
To inhibit her bliss,
For she has no history, no past,

So there she dances, eyes closed,
Head tilted back,
Leaving us all for a time,
Summoning summer joys
At will.

Hapless Sailor

I am a hapless sailor who,
Intending to mimic
The admirable, insouciant
Surefootedness of the regular crew,
Bravely signed on to the Mary Joy
To fish along the banks and bights
For the wild caught species,
For cod, haddock, sea bass
And tuna,
Yet here I lie shamefully below decks,
Moaning like a howling, baby boy,
As the mountainous swells and inhospitable winds
Toss the Mary Joy about,
Pull her up, roll her down, toy with her,
Threaten to rupture her creaking hull,

I quickly succumb to a formidable fear,
Cry out for mother,
Stumble though the narrow companionways
Trying to end my misery, consider
Hurling myself into the brawling, sinister sea,
Yet when, at last, we gain safe harbor
I embroider my virgin adventure
With gilded tales of heroism and laudable daring,
And amidst fanfare am widely celebrated
And hailed along the bustling wharves and piers
As a promising young man with the seasoned
Sea legs of a true commodore,
While my mates give me the evil eye,
And, heads down, order another round.

Pairings

On the rough Atlantic side
Uncork a cabernet,
A fortified red with body
Is the way to end your day,
On the gentler bayside,
Why not a lighter white?
Something dry with hints of sky
And subtle notes of night?
On the southern Sound side
Choose a chardonnay,
A steely one, un-oaked and clean
To match the crisp, blue day,
And if you're on the islands
Select a robust wine,
Something rare with notes to spare
Of whale and gale and brine.

Old King's Highway

Peerless, primeval pathway,
Soothing, sinuous roadway,
Meandering like a gentle
Rollercoaster along the bayside
Through history, time and
Fond, personal remembrance,
Well-preserved, modern incarnation
Of a timeless, ancient route
For animals, Native Americans
And English settlers,
Most appealing, most delightful
Of our nation's seaside treks,
Most captivating on the Cape & Islands,

I seek you out every summer
As you instantly slow my breathing,
Calm my pace,
I wander up and down,
Over and around your lush length,
Your gentle curves, little rises,
Devouring your sweet surprises,
Your heartening views
Of cranberry bog, salt marsh and sea,
Your ancient towns, sea captain homes,
Brimming with history and
Wonder to myself, if it could be,
What charming cottage, pleasant spot,
Would I one day choose for me?
When any spot at all would do
If I might settle here with you.

Sea Salt On The Tongue

Teeming thoughts in the mind,
Countless cares in the heart,
When will our island vacation start?

Now in the moment, sweet scent on the breeze,
My love at my side, we laugh and we tease,

Now quiet the mind, peace hangs in the air,
Presence of rapture, absence of care,

Sea salt on the tongue, full joy in the heart,
Too soon, oh too soon,
Now time to depart.

Portable Feast

Are the glorious gifts of the sea portable?
Is the leisurely pace you slow to here transportable?
Can you take your bits of seacoast serenity
Home with you? convey them elsewhere?
Will they easily pack? preserve within the journey back?
Will there be a residue of incremental tolerance
For friends and colleagues?
If so, for how long before it fades
And the shades of winter erase your memory of her gifts?

Will there be morsels of deep relaxation left?
Will your mind remain quiet, or revert too soon
To its familiar thought-filled riot?
Will your suspension of judgment,
Certainty and formed opinion take,
Or was it merely temporary,
A fleeting, fraudulent, high summer fake?

Your memories are mobile, why not her gifts?
You travel well, why shouldn't they?
Or perhaps the sea grants its gifts
Knowing their short shelf life
Requires that you return, like a lover keenly aware
That too much early given, leaves little more to earn?

The Creatures I Became

There are very few places
One may go
Where dignity falls away,
Unlike going along
With the daily flow
Watching each word you say,

Yet there is a place familiar to all
Where the soul may have a ball,
Where inflated pomp like Humpty's
Takes a long, well-deserved fall,

And that is the beach
My inquisitive friend,
Where the surf embraces the land,
Where cooling mists and salty spray
Caress the liquefied sand,

I recall a day not long ago
When I pulled my beach chair down,
To the very spot
Where the waves rolled in,
Soon lost my formidable frown,

I sipped from a luscious concoction,
Tipped over right into a wave,
Lay down amongst the startled crowd,
Commenced to misbehave,

Prone against the tiny waves,
I soon had a watery thought,
This must be the very paradise
All wiser men have sought,

Half naked, slightly bonkers,
Free from prudence and rules,
I made fun, fishy noises,
Swam in aquatic schools,

I mimicked a portly, slapping seal,
A slithering crocodile,
Crawled around on my belly
In true British, bedlamite style,

I was willingly witless,
Daringly daft,
Afflicted with watery joy,
I imagine I often behaved that way
When I was a very young boy,

They claim that every single year
We cycle from high to low,
Perhaps our volatile weather's
To blame as up and down we go,

Yet the apex of every year for me
Were the creatures I became,
When for a time I thankfully lost
All decorum, pride and shame.

Anchors Aweigh

Votary

I was never so light as I was by the sea,
They called me her votary,
I was never so fair in complexion as there,
As ruddy as one man could be,
I was never so tall without shoes, socks and all,
As unshod I rambled on sand,
I was never so free as a human could be,
Divorced from all chain of command,
I am never so wistful as when I recall
Summer memories that rise in the fall,
Of the person I was some few months ago,
So light, so free, so tall.

Truro In November

Middle child of the aging year,
Craving love, instilling fear
Of cold and too much thought,
For deep acquaintance seldom sought,
Coming in on bracing wind
And seaborne chill,
Introverted yet with a will
To see the year out,
Wandering among denuded trees
In alliance with whatever frees
Leaves from their branches,
Tall and hunched in a gray frock coat,
Collar up against the blast
North Atlantic storms have cast,
Filling patchy skies with fowl,
Hooded face beneath a cowl,
Preceded by a favored child,
An autumn month of colors wild,
Followed by another pet,
December's festive, feeling days and yet
You are as wondrous as your kin,
Though you will never win
With easy beauty,
Seeing yours requires patience
And a duty to look more closely,
He never acknowledged me,
Glanced over one broad shoulder

At Truro's towering dunes,
And with a stoic iron will
Was soon atop the farther hill.

Lighthouse Beach

The bravest man I ever saw
And the loneliest,
Stood tall above the majestic beach
Staring at the wintry scene
With uncommon dignity and
Old fashioned, Yankee self-restraint,
I knew unless I spoke to him
He would not speak to me,
A look-away nod at most,
He was dressed for biting winter
That crisp day, bundled head to foot
In the deepest sorrow,
Which poured from him
Down along the snow-encrusted beach,
We chatted briefly, his voice tone strong,
His conversation proper, his words few,
Not too familiar, I couldn't look him
In the eye or stand too close,
His eyes never met mine
For I knew, before he told me so,
That his wife of many years
Had recently died, that he lived
Alone, that he often stood here
On this memory laden rise
Dispersing silent sorrows
Down along the sand
Into the cold, indifferent sea,
I bid him goodbye in the unemotional,
Heartbreaking, unsatisfactory

New England way, then
Left him there, eternally adrift,
Bravest and loneliest man I ever saw.

Life's A Beach

Your seconds are her grains of sand,
Your heart sounds in her waves,
Your moods are mirrored in her sky
And how her light behaves,
Your span erodes much like her shore,
Her crescent shape, life's arc,
Your joys embodied in her sun,
Your fears within her shark,
Your youth much like swift summer flies
And like migrating birds,
Your children tender sad goodbyes
With tear-inducing words,
Your love is like the smitten sun's
Who took a shine to moon,
Like his, your love will end one day,
Quit the heart too soon,
Like you she wakes in cheery tone
With crowds, commotion, fun,
At end of day you're all alone,
Soft setting like her sun.

Before The Wind

We always raced to the Cape,
Then along the beach, up to the snack bar,
Into the water, back to the clam shack,
Before the wind, off the coast,
Out to the buoy, round the kettle pond,
Across the deck, along the breakwater,
Back to the car, down the dunes,
Around the yard, into the pool,
After the kids, along the wharf,
Up the drive, down the market aisle,
Through the lot, up the lighthouse,
Along the bike trail,
As fast as love and laughter
Could take us without fail,
Until one day she outran me,
Looked round to find me gone,
All alone ran on.

These Are The Sands

These are the sands we strolled along,
These are the waves we swam,
This is the same magnanimous sky
Made me the man I am,

These are the winds toyed with her hair,
Here were the castles we built,
This is the shore that nursed our dreams,
Our wild and crazy quilt,

These are the shells I chose for her,
Smooth stones she gifted me,
This is the place I go to confront
Death's hollow victory,

These are the dunes we lay upon
When pretty, young and free,
This is the heart still longs for her,
Alone and solitary.

Forsythia Season On The Cape

In bloom again in gay display
Along back roads and fields
Down our way are the forsythia,
How you loved these golden bells,
Lemon yellow in the dells,
Woods and yards, casting spells
To welcome spring,
Give our warblers cause to sing,
How you loved their pride and joy,
The way their tendrils did deploy,
Like pyrotechnics all around,
Freeze-frame sparklers lacking sound,
Floral fireworks on the ground,
How they circle round the trees,
Caress the stony walls,
Gently sway with every breeze
As each to sleeping brethren calls
To bloom as they do now,
Their companions in repose,
The peony, the gorgeous rose,
How you loved their simple cheer,
Their optimism for the year,
How I love their bright surprise,
Now seen through my lost lover's eyes.

Who Are These

Who are these who lie nearby?
Sun and tan beneath this sky?
Laugh and shout, run and dive,
Who are they within this hive?
Those who follow with the tide
When the tide is out?
Retreat up the sand
When the tide is in?
The tall, the short,
The stout, the thin?
And those curious solitaries,
Sitting upright head in a book
On the damp flats in a chair
With its own umbrella?
Who are these?

They are the universe's
Motley multitudes
Who merit your compassion,
With timed and tattered hearts,
Battered like you by life,
Too aware of impending death,
Stealing precious moments of peace
And transient tranquility,
Before their harried hearts beat out,
Trying hard not to think,
Hoping to keep their minds at bay
For one more day,
Praying to make this beach day last
Before they all become the past.

With Nature In Her Stead

I live alone yet am not lonely,
Ever since my one and only,
Leaving me to live
With nature in her stead, now
All new loves to me are dead,

This sea breeze,
Gentler than a new love's touch,
What need have I for such a crutch?
This Cape rain,
More soothing than a new love's speech,
What can new words this old heart reach?
Cape sun,
Warmer than a lover's embrace,
Why now should I love's arrow chase?
Cape's cozy chill,
Her spring's lush bloom,
Leave for new loves little room,

Come nurturing nature,
Hold me for the while,
All my sorrows reconcile,
Summon her memory
With all of your beauty,
Not an unfamiliar duty,

I live alone yet am not lonely,
Ever since my one and only.

The Wide Icarian Sea

Now like the father he is myth,
He danced upon the air,
A handsome boy of tender years,
His impulse go and dare,
His father was a craftsman
Who lent the boy his wings,
They shared a heedless impulse,
Won the fate such brings,
His mother knew but did not live
To save him from himself,
One day he set a fatal course
Along the coastal shelf,
The gods that day weren't watching,
He tumbled from the sky,
Perhaps the twilight and the sun
Had tricked both mind and eye,
He drowned within a skipping stone
Of mother's cliff retreat,
A much loved, daring, elder son
Whom life could not defeat,
Also lost that tragic day
Two sisters in the deep,
Who fell to earth with John John,
In god's broad arms now sleep,
They call the waters here the Sound,
Well known to you and me,
Cleaved hearts prefer another name,
The Wide Icarian Sea.

You May My Love Remember Me

When you sun upon our beach
And I am then beyond your reach,
Alone, looking out to sea,
You may my love remember me,
When you do, may your heart mend,
When you enjoy all I will send:
White-capped waves that crest and fall,
Warming zephyrs over all,
Cotton clouds above the sea,
Whiskered seals swimming free,
Soaring gulls, skittish fish,
All those things you will wish
We might still enjoy as two,
Were I not beyond your view,
Shimmering sands, sailing boats,
Laughing children, puffy floats,
Spitting clams, bright blue crabs,
Young men flaunting muscled abs,
Umbrellas flapping on the shore,
Rainbow bright, yet still more,
Warming rays, sea-polished stones,
Driftwood left like ancient bones,
Starfish that fell just last night,
A most strange and magical sight,
Upon the dunes green sea grass
That gently sways to let you pass,
A tide halfway 'tween high and low,
So once you swim you're free to go
Along that long, reflective walk

Your memory fills with all our talk,
Spread along that very sand,
When loving hand in loving hand
We strolled in bliss upon our beach,
Now well beyond your lover's reach.

Covenant

The shore and I made a pact
To help me deal with grief,
Yet what she kindly offered me
I met with disbelief,

I was to visit her each day,
Leave some grief behind,
The shore would wash away my pain,
Heal my troubled mind,

I left some sadness on the sand,
Next day my hurt the less,
Consoling tides had gifted me
With watery largesse,

Nature is a healing force
To those who seek some peace,
Though I still mourn for what I lost,
She did my woe decrease.

Reliquiae

Take these ashes, gentle breeze,
Disperse them lovingly
Along this beautiful beach,
Merge these vestiges of our beloved
With the welcoming waves,
This bracing, briny ocean air,
These shifting sands,
For the soul of our beloved
Was most at home here,
Often here took wing,
So it is fitting that these ashes
Become one with nature's splendor,
As we our dear departed now surrender,
So to you benign breeze
We now commit these cherished relics
Of our dead, for you to lovingly overspread
All along this gorgeous strand
With your benevolent hidden hand.

Cadaverous Beach

Observe closely, oblivious beachgoer,
The multitudes of dead and dying
Along this cadaverous beach,
The widely scattered, sun bleached remains
Of fish, seabirds, crustaceans,
And remind yourself that you
Will join them shortly,
Just yesterday, they were eating,
Swimming, flying, swooping,
Digging, crawling, preying,
Playing, flapping and crying,

Time now to begin saying goodbye
To yourself whatever your age,
For your identity, your precious,
Inflated, eternally unique selfhood, like theirs,
Will soon evaporate, disintegrate overnight
Into its constituent, elemental parts,
Become eternally inanimate, widely scattered,
And yes, sun bleached,
Like the scattered dead and dying here,

As you bid yourself farewell,
Acknowledge above all
Your beloved, human ephemera
Soon to pass as well,
Those special few from whom you'll part,
Held close within a dying heart.

Late Summer Plea

Not now when I have found my life,
Children, art, dear sweet wife,
Not now when I have worked it out,
The fear, the toil, the noisome doubt,
Come for those who hate their lives,
Who rage against their kids and wives,
Come for those who whine and rail,
Who shake their fist at life's fine tale,
Come sweep away those volunteers
Who manifest unconscious fears
And leave us seaside beings be,
Our lives, our home, our family,
Why contrive to truncate lives
Whose hard earned joy at last survives?
Why give us folks close scrutiny
Who never thought to bother thee?
Come take your pestilential fire,
And with your shaded confederates conspire
To reap your human harvest
In the muck and in the mire,
Just not here, not now,
When so few of us know how
To treasure life's most precious joy,
When you might others so annoy,
I pray a stay, some well-deserved delay
Before the vertiginous precipice of death,
Before the anxious culmination stops my breath,
Come cull the herd,
Disreputable and eminent alike,
Yet do not me or mine dare strike.

Chatham Bars

If death intends to find me, and
One day befriending comes to call,
At home, on mountain top,
Or deep within some urban sprawl,
I pray it find me here
On this well-favored beach,
Where this soft sand shall be my bier,
This smiling sun shall banish fear,
And these waves so crystal clear
Shall gently on their liquid backs
Convey me lovingly to the stars,
Across her shifting Chatham bars.

Fade To Fall

Where have you gone
Bold colors of summer?
Ultramarine, vermilion red,
Leaving a paler palette in their stead?
Where your vibrant richness now?
Where royal blue of stern and prow?
Where goldenrod at end of day?
Did all bright plumage fly away?
Where glowing gold of afternoon?
Prismatic rainbows born in June?
I grant we're left with tint and hue,
Fair autumn brings warm colors too,
Yet where the vivid tones we knew?
Or is it once you fade to fall
Bold colors make their curtain call?

Chapoquoit Cottage

In the gloaming came a breeze
That fluttered through the linden trees,
Moved their crowns in graceful dance,
Giving me yet another chance
To think of her whom I had lost,
What intervening years had cost,
It circled high among their tops,
Cleared a row, one small copse,
Then down across the lawn to me
To set my favorite picture free,
From where it hung upon the wall,
I watched it slowly, gently, fall,
Until at last it came to rest
At nature's true and wise behest
Right there where I stood,
My paragon of womanhood,
From out the lovely linden trees
Upon a kind, consoling, ocean breeze.

Gratitude

Whom do I thank
For eyes that see?
One unique identity?
Arms to embrace?
This time, this place?
Cape & Islands
Special grace?
Ears to hear?
This spinning sphere?
A brain to think?
A heart to heal?
An angel to wed,
Beau ideal?
Arms to enfold,
Good as gold,
And a soul aflame?
Do you have a name,
A home, a title, rank?
Tell me please
Whom do I thank?

All Your Wealth For Now

Quite soon no matter your age,
Fresh beauty or hopeful dreams of a long life,
Out there in the indifferent sea
Lies all cessation of strife and the end of life,
No matter the present vibrancy
Of your bursting heart, resolution, will to live
Or quaint certainty of a friendly fate,
Such awareness gives a start,

This vital beach, its color and clamor
And your serene soul, well beyond the reach
Of fear and trepidation, do deceive
For no reprieve is granted,
All human life is transmuted just out there
In the middle distance, in the offing,
Just beyond the anchoring ground
Where the ocean's deep, all life unsound,

Frolic here then while you can,
Babbling child, aging man,
Loiter for nothing is promised,
Be greedy for life now, gorge yourself,
Be a glutton for leisure and fun
Under a false, perennially two-faced sun,

Kiss her now, hold him now,
Not a one knows when and how,
This beach day's all your wealth
For now.

A True Nantucket Beauty

I brushed her hair
Then kissed her,
Youngest of my girls,
Ran my hands with tender care
Through all her amber curls,
Touched her dimples gently,
One cheek, then the other,
She always coyly showed them off
Much like her older brother,
Then set a bow atop her hair,
She didn't make a sound,
In her the sweetest of my girls
No care could oft be found,
Rouged her up just a touch,
Pinched so blood would flow,
Secured a shawl of Wicklow wool,
She may be chill you know,
Then a swatch of Galway lace,
Her party shoes and dress,
A true Nantucket beauty
I must to you confess,
Then lovingly placed her
Into the ground,
Into the sodden bog,
Into the welcoming,
Teeming earth,
Amidst the island fog.

A Lifeguard Whispered In My Ear

A lifeguard whispered in my ear
Discretely once or twice,
"We'll soon be sailing from the pier,"
His time was imprecise,

I set my chair upon the sand,
Spread my towel wide,
Placed thereon her favorite shells,
Waited for low tide,

I saw him next upon the sand,
Motioning me to come,
To join his little, ragtag band
Heading towards the sun,

I looked back twice to see you there,
Asleep upon the sand,
Unsuspecting, free from care,
My heart was in my hand,

I promise you that I will wait
Out there beyond the sea,
When moon and time
And friendly fate
An ebb tide send for thee.

Jean Ryan Of Brewster

There are shortcuts to happiness
So they say,
One is to dance, one is to sing,
Not long ago I danced with Jean,
Each to the other joy did bring,

She wished to live to dance that day,
Her smile gave all her bliss away,
With awkward gait, earnest step,
She matched me there with equal pep,

Lost in the dance, moving fast,
Each felt delight that could not last,
On the floor at speed of sound
We danced and flew round and round,
As if together we might forestall
The muted trumpet's final call.

I smiled at her, she beamed at me,
Each pleased such shortcuts came to be,
It may have been her final dance,
I'll never know for sure,
But when she has another chance
With dancing soul so pure,
She'll dance again, radiant, out of sight,
Illumined by angelic light,

There are shortcuts to happiness,
Joy they bring,
One is to dance, one is to sing,
Not long ago I danced with Jean,
Dancing now, sight unseen.

To My Cape & Islands

Who'll sing of you when I have gone?
Of your vibrant colors, dazzling dawn?
Who will extol, write and share,
When I am no longer there?

Most are well intentioned,
At least believe they are,
But unused to life, befuddled by it,
Overwhelmed by it, made fearful by it,
Uncertain what to make of nature
Beyond calling you a vacation or a break,
Some will awaken, credit you
With more than your due,
While others like the self-absorbed
Will use you up before they're through,

Yet who will celebrate? who will write?
Who will praise before their fated night
All your glories warm and bright?
You'll need another stalwart friend
Before your own erosive end.

Vineyard Valedictory

First life gave me animating breath,
Two guardian spirits, five acute senses to feel,
See, hear, smell and taste this favored seaside place,
A virile body to navigate what my senses found,
Then undiluted joy and play came my winsome way,
A mind to think, a heart to feel, then turned the wheel,
An angel to wed, who gave me love and pretty babies
Who smiled up at me, then turned the wheel
And life gently asked for everything back,
Quietly took in turn my guardian angels,
Gave my fledglings wings, called my soul mate home,
Reclaimed my senses one by one beneath a slowly, setting sun,
Moderated joy and play, took health in bits from day to day,
Moved my still full heart away from sweet to bittersweet,
And one momentous wintry day I ceased to think,
Ceased to feel, my precious breath sweet life did seal,
Then turned the wheel to someone new.

Looking Out To Sea

I have no need for paradise,
Though angels seem divine,
My life was blessed, full of love,
Nor do I for a heaven pine,
It seems to me this is it,
This glory 'tween two sleeps,
This earth to me a paradise
My life will not o'er leap,
My blessings came in numbers,
Too numerous to sum,
Rapture here enough for me,
A Heaven would benumb.

Beach Life

Three phases
To everyone's beach life:
The first, deeply unconscious,
Liberating, full of activity
And animal joy,
Doing, running,
Playing, laughing,
No questions,

The second, semi-conscious
Awareness of where you are,
Who you are,
Nature's art, passing time,
What it feels like
To be in a human body,
Many questions,

The third, bittersweet, replete
With recollection,
Grudging gratitude, poignancy,
Awareness of loss as the gloss
Begins to fade,
One question, one answer
In the affirmative.

Find A Safe Harbor

"Find a safe harbor," father said
Before he yawned and went to bed,
Sailed the next for parts unknown,
Now he's gone, I am grown.

"Seek a safe harbor," mother said
Before she kissed me on the head,
I watched her ketch slow sail away,
Morning of the very next day,

All my uncles uttered the same,
Neighbors, strangers too,
I searched our coastline
Far and wide,
Yet no safe harbor knew,

"Gain a safe harbor," I tell my own
Now they are full grown,
"Where shall we look?" my oldest said,
Before her father went to bed,

"It's not a place," I told her straight,
Knowing that my time was late,
"Trust your heart without fail,
At break of day I too will sail."

How Shall I Mourn Thee

How shall I mourn thee, my sweet Jack?
How shall I mourn thee dear?

With a garland of seaweed in your hair
And the dunes and the seashore near,

How shall I think of you, my sweet soul?
How shall I think of you dear?

Frolicking madly in the waves
With the sun and its rays for cheer,

How shall I grieve thee, my sweet man?
How shall I grieve thee dear?

With a potent concoction in your hand
And the thunder of waves in your ear,

Where shall I seek thee, my dear heart?
Where shall I seek thee dear?

Where the rollers rush to kiss this sand
For we were happy here.

In The Wind

When I am dead and in the wind
I will not miss the painful partings,
False friends, true enemies, all loose ends,
The relentless striving, slow decay,
Decade to decade, day to day,

I will not miss the sudden betrayals,
My febrile, untamable mind,
Those disconcerting things you find
In the morning news,
Which do the tender soul abuse,

Yet I will miss god's great, blue earth,
All fine nature which from birth
I found a friend,
From my inception to my end,
And you beside me here offshore,
Soaked with sea spray,
Serenaded by the whistling winds
And clanging rigging,

When I am dead and in the breeze,
The only thoughts that will appease
Will be of you and this transcendent
Offshore view.

Wellfleet Harbor

Let's conspire to slip away
From where our love's now moored,
Devise some sultry, summer day
A plan to cut the cord
That binds us to this harbor,
Anchors us to place and
Free our love to roam the earth
Upon its liquid face,
Let's celebrate our sailing days
Beneath a cheery sun,
Make love beneath the spangled stars,
All anchorage to shun,
Let's form an intrigue very soon,
A scheme, a perfect plot
And seek that boundless, open place
Remorseless time forgot,
There to wander after time
All other loves has ended,
Aware that we alone on earth
Have time's fell hand suspended.

Closed For The Season

The mind at play,
Soul that danced day on day,
Seaside memory making,
Zen of an amiable sea
There for the taking,
Reality that matched the anticipation,
The striking colors of summer,
Limitless panoramas,
The ecstasy of no schedule,
The apex of the psyche's year,
Banishment of both regret and fear,
Surest fix for a leaden mood,
The body's textile freedom,
The effortless healing, easy joys,
Seaside play of girls and boys,
Fragrant breezes
And for those it pleases
The mucking about in boats,
Newly awakened taste buds,
Bobbing, rainbow-colored floats,
The yearned for lightness of being,
The sloughing off of the heavy toll
The year between has taken,
Closed for the season,
Beyond all rhyme or reason.

From Off The Beach

Transient gust
From off the beach,
Faint flutter
Of a half-pulled shade,
Distant tinkling
Of a rusted wind chime,
A pale, much loved
Slender hand
That fell away from mine
And she was gone,
And with her
Our home's bright bouquet,
Its only breathable air,
Sole lyric to my temporal song,
My one life's touchstone
And in her cherished place
A treasure chest of memories,
Torrents of private tears,
An aging man now set adrift,
Prey to rising fears.

To Keep Your Eyes On Me

As I go, when I go,
I will hand you my sunglasses,
Broad brimmed sunhat,
Faded, blue tee shirt,
Blue-green, striped beach towel
And as before
Will stumble backwards
Into the lime-green waves
Grinning at you standing there,
Wearing my hat, holding my things,
And I will perform for you
All the way in
Without turning once
To face the covetous sea,
Diving this way and that,
Falling as if wounded,
Muttering silly things
As the distance between us grows,
Shuddering, as if nipped by a shark,
Yelping, as if pinched by a crab,
Falling backwards,
Flailing in the water, mugging,
Anything to keep your eyes on me
As I go, when I go,
And my last thoughts
Will all be of you smiling there
A few feet into the sparkling surf,

Sending your affectionate beams
One last time my way
To make the glaring sun jealous
And the cresting waves
To dance with envy.

Make Me A Castle On The Sand

Father make me a castle on the sand
Whose fortress walls will all withstand
The force of waves and fickle fate
And not in time disintegrate,
Make me a citadel, father dear,
To shield from surging surf and fear,
Whose ramparts will keep me safe, secure,
Whose battlements will reassure,

Daughter I made you a castle on the sand
With thickset walls to waves withstand,
Carved a trench full deep and wide
Behind which child you might hide,
But fathers like walls are made of sand,
No father can all waves withstand,
No matter their efforts, one fine day,
Fathers too will fall away.

One Last Taste Of The Sea

Before I go,
One last taste of the sea,
The touch of sand against bare feet,
Things that meant the most to me,
Feel of spray upon my face,
One last goodbye to this fine place,
The sight of dunes upon the rise,
A final treat for aging eyes,
A glimpse of sails upon the sea,
The knowing you are near to me,
Warm midday sun upon my chest
And for the best you here beside,
Before I go you should know
I found a heaven here with you,
Where sand and sea
Our love made new.

The Jetty

I watched my love and she watched me
As year-by-year we ceased to be
What each had been when life was full
And each could pull their weight
And never hesitate,

I watched my love and she watched me
As day by day the will to be
Receded for her, receded for me,
Our babes had grown, long since flown,
Our debts had long been paid,

I watched my love and in her eyes
I found a look of sad surprise,
She saw the same in mine,
In silence each had come
To this same thought sublime:
We'll go together my love and I,

So one morn to her I said
As she lay in bed,
"Are your ready, dear?"
"I am ready," she replied softly,
"I'll remember your voice,"
"And I your smile,"
"Come take my hand,"
"I have your hand,"
"Now on my count,
Jump, my love,
Jump."

Ebb Tide

Now at last to sleep,
No more promises
Save one to keep,
To wake if wake we do
Only in a world where you
Are waiting, anticipating,
No other world, no other time
Or place for me
If your adoring eyes I will not see,
If not, let me slumber for eternity,

What kind of angel are you?
Faithfully watched over me,
Made of my life a happy place,
Now see me off with easy grace?
A queen of angels,
Archangel in command of cohorts,
Or a kind solitary doing divine bidding
In small, broken places
Like the wounded hearts of men?

Come let my arms enfold you
One last time,
These now thin, unmuscled arms,
Greedy yet for all your charms,
Let my heart's last beats sound there
In synchrony with yours.

Last Offices

Early September, morning air now chill,
Fuller bodied, dimpling the skin,
The waking sun assumes a lower track,
My bedroom aerie is naturally,
Miraculously, air-conditioned,
All of this presaging the youth of fall,
Signaling the slow death
Of fast ripening, senescent summer,

I reluctantly don a light robe, mourn
The loss of bone-invasive heat,
The calming cadence of gentle waves,
The regenerative potency of the shoreline,
The maritime merriment of summer
And the joyful yet brief emancipation
Of the body from the prison house
Of cloth and weave,

Days will be cozier now,
Retreating skies higher,
Memories more intrusive,
As I mourn the loss of high summer
And its surpassing joys now elusive,
Yet I shall conduct my obsequies
With propriety despite my sadness,
And with a pious reverence perform
The last, solemn offices due the brief,
Shimmering, midyear majesty
Of our brilliant and bountiful
Season of sun.

Cape Light

More light as I get older,
More sun, wider views,
Broader vistas, brighter blues,
As my world closes in,
Time quickens and
The end games begin,

More light,
As I advance in years,
Less shade, higher skies,
More unobstructed views,
More sunny days, longer days,
Less cloud cover, little rain,
And if you please
More open space,

More light as I age,
As I turn life's
Penultimate page,
More lovely, limitless,
Life-enhancing light,
Cape light.

Sea Breezes

We blow in on the breath of an onshore breeze,
Depart on the breath of her brother,
We discover the sand, the sea and the shore,
Well nurtured by father and mother,
We play for a time 'neath the sun and the rain,
Our span filled with joy, tinged with loss,
And into the breeze that rustles the trees
Our unanswered questions we toss,

Some decide their time was a blessing,
Others bemoan they blew in,
While most of us just keep on guessing,
Might questioning life be a sin?
We depart on the breath of an offshore breeze,
Some grateful, others uncertain,
Skimming above the white-capped waves
Towards a slowly opening curtain.

Arrow Heart & All

He wrote her name upon the sand,
Added there his own,
Encircled each with loving hand
Within the tidal zone,
Every day she walked the beach
Her smiling eyes would fall
Down upon their sunlit names
Arrow, heart and all,
At times he wrote with driftwood
Or spelled her name with shells,
Yet every time he wrote her name
It faded with the swells,
I watched him write, I saw her beam,
I often walked behind,
What must their life consist of,
Two lovers of one mind?
One summer day he went away,
He'd reached a certain age,
No names upon the pristine sand,
A bare and empty page,
When next I saw her searching
I felt a twinge of pain,
She would not find her name again
Or his along the plain,
Yet when the tide receded
I saw upon her face
A smile of recognition
His death could not erase,
For on that spot her name appeared,

Arrow, heart and all,
As did his and as I neared
I marveled at it all,
He wrote her name upon the sand,
Added there his own,
Encompassed each with loving hand,
There the sunlight shone.

Prayer Of A Summer Night

Gentle me now, shield me from light,
Guide me into Your nourishing night,
Send through my window Your fresh sea air,
One flickering star make prominent there,
Hang a full moon above those trees,
Round and gilt as cheddar cheese,
Take all of my errant thoughts away,
Countless cares of the fading day,
I've written them here, every one,
I hand them to You, my day is done,
Convey my love to all in my care,
From pain and sorrow each one spare,
Slow my breathing, close my eyes,
Grant me all bright day denies,
Sleep me deeply till break of day,
This I pray, this I pray.

Beach Blessing

May you come into a cottage
By the sea,
May you never own a boat,
May your sand be soft and silken,
May a benign sun warm your skin,
The cooling sea welcome you in,
When one day you weigh anchor,
May a genial, offshore breeze
Billow your sails.

'Night Cape
& Islands

Quite late,
Soul mate,
First rate,
Clean slate,
Joy rife,
No strife,
Long life,
Sound fife,
Sleepy head,
Snug abed,
'Nuff said,
Peace to all,
Nightfall,
Ship shape,
'Night Cape
& Islands

75448623R00262

Made in the USA
San Bernardino, CA
30 April 2018